LB
2842
.C58   B 333264

Teachers' Salaries in New York City

Final Report
OF THE
Citizens Committee on Teachers Salaries

DISTRIBUTED BY
BUREAU OF PUBLICATIONS
TEACHERS COLLEGE, COLUMBIA UNIVERSITY
NEW YORK CITY
1927

PRICE $1.25

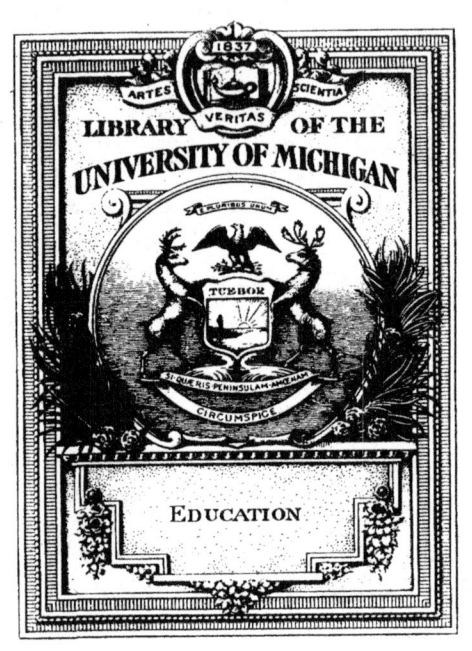

Teachers' Salaries in New York City

Final Report
OF THE
Citizens Committee on Teachers Salaries

Robert E. Simon, Chairman
Marinobel Smith, Executive Secretary

James R. McGaughy, Director

DISTRIBUTED BY
BUREAU OF PUBLICATIONS
TEACHERS COLLEGE, COLUMBIA UNIVERSITY
NEW YORK CITY
1927

LB
2842
.C58

Educ.
Wahr.
7-1-29
19898

CITIZENS' COMMITTEE ON TEACHERS' SALARIES

Robert E. Simon, Chairman
Dr. J. R. McGaughy, Director
George J. Hecht, Treasurer
Marinobel Smith, Executive Secretary

Executive Committee

Mrs. Seymour Barnard
William C. Breed
Miss Martha L. Draper
E. W. Edwards
John H. Finley
Lee K. Frankel
George J. Hecht
Raymond V. Ingersoll
Charles C. Lockwood
John Martin
Mrs. Henry Moskowitz
Mrs. George V. Mullan
Lawson Purdy
Nelson S. Spencer
Percy S. Straus
Mrs. Joseph Swan

General Committee

Richard B. Aldcroft
Mrs. Rogers H. Bacon
Mrs. Francis McNeil Bacon
Charles B. Barnes
Alfred M. Barrett
Robert F. Binkerd
Mrs. John Blair
Mrs. Linsee Blagden
Mrs. H. Blaskopf
Bruce Bliven
Meyer Bloomfield
Alfred C. Bosson
Mrs. Frank H. Bottemus
Dr. S. Parkes Cadman
Mrs. Joseph T. P. Callahan
Newcomb Carlton
Sydney S. Cohen
Martin Conboy
Joseph P. Cotton
John Coughlin
Mrs. A. W. Courtney
Mrs. Frederick L. Cranford
James Curtis
Mrs. Joseph Griswold Deane
Leopold Demuth
Mrs. H. Edward Dreier
Dr. Louis I. Dublin

Frederick H. Ecker
Mrs. Abram I. Elkus
Dr. John Elliott
Mrs. F. S. Enger
Mrs. W. E. Evans
Miss Gertrude I. Ferre
Dr. George J. Fisher
Dr. Henry Fleischman
Miss Mary Frasca
Mrs. Howard S. Gans
Dr. C. J. Celler
Mrs. Charles Dana Gibson
Rabbi Herbert S. Goldstein
I. Edwin Goldwasser
Maurice Goodman
Samuel Greenbaum
Mrs. Simon Guggenheim
Stanley E. Gunnison
Mrs. Otto Hahn
Charles E. Heitman
Mrs. Anna W. Hochfelder
Ralph Jonas
Otto H. Kahn
Francis I. Ketcham
Miss Mabel Hyde Kittredge
Mrs. Alexander Kohut
Dr. Nathan Krass

Mrs. James Lees Laidlaw
Mrs. Charles Lested
Bishop Wm. T. Manning
Mrs. Andrew V. Markey
Mrs. Park Mathewson
Alexander A. Mayper
Mrs. Wm. Brown Meloney
Darwin J. Messerole
Wm. J. Morris, Jr.
John G. Murray
Mrs. Frederick Nathan
Mrs. Karl Nelson
Dr. Henry Neumann
Mrs. G. O'Connor
Arthur Pleydell
John A. Poynton
Joseph M. Price
Mrs. Miriam Sutro Price
Mrs. Joseph M. Proskauer
Mrs. W. H. Reh
Mrs. Douglas Robinson
S. G. Rosenbaum
Wm. Bradford Roulstone
Mrs. Anna Rumph
Frederick C. Schmid
Mrs. Thomas K. Schmuck

CITIZENS' COMMITTEE ON TEACHERS SALARIES'

General Committee
Continued

Bernard Schwarts
Dr. Albert Shiels
Morris Sigman
Mrs. Charles E. Simonson
Mrs. William Singer
Barry K. Smith
Morton Stein
Mrs. M. I. Stich
Mrs. W. E. Whitlock Stokes
Mrs. Stephen Story
Lionel Sutro
Mrs. Lionel Sutro
Mrs. Ordway Tead
Mrs. Charles L. Tiffany
Herbert K. Twitchell
Mrs. Coffin Van Rensselaer
Richard Welling
Mrs. Rosalie Loew Whitney
Arthur Williams
Dr. Stephen S. Wise

TABLE OF CONTENTS

CHAPTER		PAGE
	Summary of a Study of Teachers' Salaries in the New York City Public Schools	1
I	Historical Review of the Teacher Salary Situation	7
	Salary Legislation Prior to 1900	8
	The Ahearn Bills of 1898-1899	8
	The Davis Bill of 1900	9
	The Equal Pay Campaign	10
	The Gaynor Commission	11
	Lockwood-Donohue Bill of 1920	12
	The Ricca Bill of 1925-1926	14
	The Friedsam Commission	15
	The Citizens' Committee on Teachers' Salaries Organized	16
	The Second Ricca Bill, 1926	17
II	Plan of Attack	20
	A. The Purchasing Power of Teachers' Salaries in 1926	21
	B. Teacher Salary Increases Compared with Increases of Other Wages and Salaries	28
	C. Teachers' Salaries in New York City and in Other Large American Cities	29
	D. Economic and Professional Status of New York City Teachers	30
	E. Attractiveness of New York City Salaries to Outside Teachers	45
III	The Facts Discovered	47
	A. Relative Purchasing Power of 1926 Salaries	48
	B. Increases in Teachers' Salaries Compared with those in Wages and Other Salaries	56
	C. Salaries in Other Large American Cities	61
	D. The Professional and Economic Status of New York City Teachers	64

TABLE OF CONTENTS
(continued)

CHAPTER		PAGE
III (continued)	Amount of Professional Preparation	66
	Amount of Teaching Experience	72
	A Study of Teachers' Dependents	75
	Number of Children of Married Teachers	84
	The Earnings of New York City Teachers	84
	Annual Rentals Paid By New York City Teachers	89
	Expenditures for Food	95
	E. Attractiveness of New York City Salaries to Outside Teachers	100
IV	The Basic Assumptions	102
	A. Commonly Accepted Bases for Schedules	102
	The Single Salary Schedule	104
	Teacher Rating as a Salary Basis	107
	Salary Differentials Based on Sex of Teacher	108
	Age or Grade of Children Taught	109
	Amount of Teaching Experience	114
	Kind and Amount of Professional Preparation	115
	Ability to Pass Teachers Examinations	118
	The Number of Dependents or Size of Family	120
	Educational Achievement of Pupils	121
	Number of Hours of Teaching Service	123
	The Law of Supply and Demand	125
	B. Characteristics of the Plan Adopted	128
	Characteristics of the "First Step" Proposed	135
V	Procedures Used in Determining Schedules	140
	Summary of the Principles Accepted	140
	Actual Determination of Schedules	144
	Schedule for Senior High School Teachers	144
	Schedule for Elementary School Teachers	152
	Schedule for Junior High School and Grades 7 to 9	157
	Teachers of Atypical Children	161

TABLE OF CONTENTS
(continued)

CHAPTER   PAGE

V (continued)   Training School Teachers 162
                    Senior High School First Assistants.. 163
                    Elementary School Principals 165
                    Senior High School Principals 168
                    Junior High School Principals 169
                    Assistants to Elementary Principals.. 170
                    Other Administrative and Supervisory
                        Officers 172
                    Schedules for Special Types of
                        Schools 178
                    Per Diem Schedules 180

VI   The Proposed Schedules 181
          Summary of Proposed Salary Schedules 182
          A. Schedules for Teachers in Regular Day
              Schools 182
          B. Schedules for Principals and Other
              Administrative Officers of
              Regular Day Schools 183
          C. Schedules for Positions in Special Schools.. 184
          D. Schedules for General Administrative and
              Supervisory Officers 184a
          E. Per Diem Schedules 185-187
          Cost of the Proposed Schedules 189

VII   The Committee's Publicity and Outcomes of Its
          Study 196
          The Publicity Program 203
          Informing the Committee - The First Step 205
          The Committee Vs. the Public School Teacher
              and Administrator 207
          The Mayor's Commission on Teachers' Salaries ... 219

Appendix A
    Detailed Statistical Tables 223

Appendix B
    Schedules of Ricca-Strauss Bill of 1926 252

TABLES

NUMBER		PAGE
I	Computation of Indexes of Cost of Living	51
II	Estimated Cost for 1927 of Proposed Schedules	191

APPENDIX

III	Changes in Cost of Living in New York City from December 1914 to December 1925	224
IV	Index Numbers Showing the Trend in the Retail Cost of Food in the United States, By Years, 1890 to 1925	225
V	Relative Purchasing Power of Teachers' Salaries of 1910 and 1925 Men Teachers of New York City	226
VI	Relative Purchasing Power of Teachers' Salaries of 1910 and 1925 – Women Teachers of New York City	227
VII	Relative Purchasing Power of Teachers' Salaries of 1910 and 1925 – Men and Women Teachers of New York City	228
VIII	Index for 1925 Salaries Based on the Purchasing Power of the 1900 Dollar	229
IX	Facts Concerning Salaries in New York City and In Six Other American Cities	230
X	The Professional Preparation of New York City Teachers	233

APPENDIX (continued)

NUMBER		PAGE
XI	Amount of Teaching Experience of New York City Teachers	256
XII	Dependents of Certain Groups of Women Teachers Classified as to Economic Status	238
XIII	Relationship of Years of Teaching Service to Numbers of Dependents	239
XIV	Relationship Between Number of Children and Number of Dependents of Married Men Teachers	241
XV	Teachers' Earnings From All Sources	242
XVI	The Relationship of Earnings of Married Men Teachers to Number of Children in Family	244
XVII	Rents Paid and Sub-Rents Received by New York City Teachers	245
XVIII	Rents Paid and Sub-Rents Received by Men and Women Teachers	246
XIX	Rentals of Different Types of Housing Accomodations.	247
XX	Average Annual Rentals Paid by Several Salary Groups	248
XXI	Monthly Expense for Meals	249
XXII	Relationship of Number of Children to Monthly Expense for Meals	251
XXIII	Rents Paid by Several Teaching Groups	251a
XXIV	Strauss-Ricca Bill - Salary Schedules for New York City Teachers	253

CHARTS

NUMBER		PAGE
1	Relationship of Index of Retail Cost of Food in United States from 1900 to 1925 and Index of Total Cost of Living in New York City from 1914 to 1925	24
2	Reproduction of Copy of Inquiry Blank - Voluntary Confidential Report to the Citizens' Committee on Teachers' Salaries	32
3	Reproduction of Duplicate Copy of Inquiry Blank	36
4	Two Composite Indexes of Wages in the United States	57
5	Index of Teachers' Salaries in the United States Compared with Composite Index of Wages in the United States	60
6	Per Cents of Men and Women Teachers Having Indicated Number of Persons Chiefly Dependent On Their Incomes	77
7	Per Cents of Women Teachers Having Indicated Numbers of Persons Chiefly Dependent On Their Incomes	80
8	Per Cents of Men Teachers Having Indicated Number of Persons Chiefly Dependent on Their Incomes	81
9	Relationship of Size of Family to Monthly Expense for Meals	97
10	Diagram Illustrating Proposed Plan for Salary Schedule	135
11	Publicity Program	198
12	Typical Headlines	204
13	Excerpts from "School and Society" and "The New York Teacher"	210
14	Editorials	214-215
	Selected Captions	222a
	1910 Value of Teachers' Pay	222b
	Selected Editorials	222c

SUMMARY OF A STUDY OF TEACHERS' SALARIES
IN THE NEW YORK CITY PUBLIC SCHOOLS

Teachers' salaries in New York City have been in a large measure the football of politics for the last thirty years. Except as a result of mandatory legislation the Board of Education has increased the salaries of teachers only once during this whole period. As a rule, increases in salaries have been secured through the political pressure brought upon the Legislature by organizations of the teachers themselves. The salary bills which have been passed by the Legislature have been the creatures of compromise among competing groups of teachers. The test of a good salary bill has been its ability to command the support of the several contending factions among the teachers. The scientific soundness of the provisions of a salary bill has not been accepted as essential.

The Citizens' Committee on Teachers' Salaries was organized to provide a service to the teachers and to the community. The sole purpose of its organization was to determine the facts concerning teachers' salaries and to take salary adjustments out of politics by recommending fair and equitable schedules which could be accepted by citizens and teachers alike. It was not organized as a salary-raising committee but as a fact-finding commission.

There were four essential elements in the Committee's organization. One was the choice of an Executive Committee of about 15 members. This group was small enough that it could meet together and discuss in detail and reach conclusions concerning the many complicated problems involved in a study of teachers' salaries. The second element was the choice of a Director who could be held responsible for carrying out the details of the technical and professional studies undertaken by the Committee. The third feature of the organization was the choice of an Advisory Committee of economic and statistical specialists to pass upon the validity of the studies undertaken by the Director for the Committee. Fourth, and very important, was the selection of an Executive Secretary who was given charge of publicity and the securing of money to finance the Committee's work. This person acted as the connecting link between the Committee and the public.

The Committee decided upon and carried through a fivefold plan of attack on the problem of teachers' salaries. One study had to do with the relation of present salaries to those paid earlier in New York City, on the bases of their purchasing power. The second study was that of the comparative increases in teachers' salaries in New York City and in the wages and salaries of other employed groups during recent years. A third study was made of the bases for paying salaries and the amounts of salary paid in other large American cities, and the fourth attack upon the problem was a detailed study of the professional and economic status of the New York City teachers as revealed by 11,000 voluntary confidential reports filled out by individual teachers in the New York City public schools. The fifth study was that of the degree to which the salaries and teaching conditions in New York City were attracting teachers from outside the city.

The results of these five studies convinced the Citizens' Committee that the present salaries of teachers in New York City should be increased and that certain groups should receive a larger percentage of increase than should others. The facts which led to these conclusions are presented in some detail in Chapter III and in the statistical tables in Appendix A, page 223, of the report which follows.

The Citizens' Committee was soon forced to the conclusion that it could not hope to improve the conditions which were discovered by these five studies unless it made definite recommendations to the Board of Education with respect to salary schedules and bases for paying teachers.

In arriving at the recommendations presented in this report the Committee gave careful consideration to many suggested bases for determining the salary of teachers. It discarded as unsound or impracticable all of these bases except four. The bases which were accepted by the Committee as valid and practicable are these:

(1) The number of years of teaching experience;

(2) The amount and kind of technical and professional training;

(3) Under certain conditions, the ability of teachers to pass examinations set by the Board of Education, and

(4) The operation of the economic law of supply and demand if it be so applied as to safeguard certain social and professional values.

Among features of salary schedules which were rejected by the Committee were these:

(1) Higher pay for men than for women teachers;

(2) Higher pay for teachers of older children or of more advanced grades;

(3) Higher pay for teachers rated as superior by their supervisory officers, and

(4) The "family" wage, or higher salaries for teachers having greater numbers of dependents.

The Committee found it impracticable to recommend the immediate adoption of salary schedules based solely upon the four factors which it accepted as sound and practicable indexes of teaching ability because of the fact that the Board of Education does not have available detailed information concerning the present status of the professional training of individual teachers. It is therefore recommended that not later than 1930 New York City school teachers shall begin to be paid solely on the basis of their professional qualifications for the educational positions which they hold. The most common name for the plan which the Committee recommends for adoption not later than 1930 is that of "single salary schedule", but this name is inaccurate and misleading.

The salary situations discovered in the studies of the Committee were such that the Committee was under the necessity of recommending for immediate adoption a first step in salary adjustment. The characteristics by which the first step proposed by the Committee differs from the present plan of paying teachers in New York City are four in number: (1) It is proposed that the salaries of practically all groups of teachers and administrative and supervisory officers be increased at once; (2) it is proposed that all annual salaries shall be evenly divisible by twelve (12) in order that the book-keeping of the Board of Education may be simplified and made less expensive; (3) it is proposed that there shall be small annual increments for the first three or four years of service under each schedule for teachers and that these shall be followed by substantially larger increments to all teachers who have been longer in service; and (4) the Committee proposes that a super-maximum salary shall be paid to all regular teachers who have secured as much as one year of approved professional preparation beyond the standard minimum qualifications for their licenses.

In determining the schedules for senior high school teachers, married men with a wife and one child were accepted as the basic group. In the case of elementary teachers unmarried women living away from home were accepted as basic. These two schedules were accepted as fundamental and other schedules were determined largely on the basis of relative salaries paid to corresponding professional groups in other large American cities.

The basic group used in determining each of the schedules mentioned above was the indispensable professional group whose living cost was highest. It was through application of this principle - that all teachers on a given schedule should be paid enough that the indispensable group could live comfortably and decently - that women living away from home, and married men, respectively, were used in determining the schedules proposed for elementary school and senior high school teachers. It was further accepted by the Committee that the average cost of food and rent should not exceed 55 per cent of the basic salary for each teaching group.

The detailed schedules recommended by the Committee are reported in Chapter VI, pages 181 to 195.

ROBERT E. SIMON, CHAIRMAN
DR. J. R. MC GAUGHY, DIRECTOR
GEORGE J. HECHT, TREASURER
MARINOBEL SMITH, EXECUTIVE SECRETARY

CITIZENS COMMITTEE ON TEACHERS SALARIES
1457 BROADWAY
ROOM 804
NEW YORK CITY
TEL. WISCONSIN 3131

EXECUTIVE COMMITTEE
MRS. SEYMOUR BARNARD
WILLIAM C. BREED
MISS MARTHA L. DRAPER
E. W. EDWARDS
JOHN H. FINLEY
LEE K. FRANKEL
RAYMOND V. INGERSOLL
CHARLES C. LOCKWOOD
JOHN MARTIN
MRS. HENRY MOSKOWITZ
MRS. GEORGE V. MULLAN
LAWSON PURDY
NELSON B. SPENCER
PERCY S. STRAUS
MRS. JOSEPH SWAN

ADVISORY COMMITTEE
DONALD R. BELCHER
DR. LOUIS I. DUBLIN
PROF. WILLFORD I. KING
DR. ALBERT SHIELS

LETTER OF TRANSMITTAL

To the Board of Education and to the Citizens of New York City:

    The Citizens' Committee on Teachers Salaries submits herewith the final report of its study of teachers' salaries in New York City.

    Believing that it would be a genuine service to the Board of Education, to the teachers and to the general public of New York City, and to the cause of public education, to make an impartial, fact-finding study of the vexing problems of teachers' salaries, the Citizens' Committee was organized and has functioned for that sole purpose. The work of the Committee has been financed entirely through the voluntary contributions of interested citizens. It is under no obligation of any sort to any civic, professional or political organization.

    Early in its work the Committee was forced to the conclusion that it would be wasteful and futile simply to report a mass of facts concerning the professional and economic status of New York City teachers. It has therefore translated these facts into the proposals for changed bases of paying teachers and the recommendations as to definite salary schedules which are here reported.

    The Committee makes no claim that this report has said the last word concerning teachers' salaries in New York City. It does report the best solutions which could be reached by a group of serious-minded citizens who have devoted some months of time and some thousands of dollars to an honest effort to serve the children and teachers and citizens of this community.

    The Committee hopes that this report may be the basis for an early adjustment of teachers' salaries in New York City.

Respectfully submitted,
CITIZENS' COMMITTEE ON TEACHERS' SALARIES
Robert E. Simon, Chairman

January 17, 1927.

CHAPTER I

HISTORICAL REVIEW OF THE TEACHER SALARY SITUATION

The Board of Education is appointed by the Mayor to represent the public in administering the Department of Public Education in New York City. It is the function, therefore, of the Board of Education to establish teacher salary schedules. But, for the past thirty years the method of financing public education in New York has led to a division of responsibility between the City Board of Estimate and Apportionment and the Board of Education.

As may be seen from the following history of salary legislation the Board of Education has several times during this period proposed salary changes for which the Board of Estimate has refused appropriations. This dual financial control has made it difficult to fix the responsibility for teachers' salaries with the Board of Education. The teachers, perforce, turned to Albany for salary adjustment, introducing their own bills for salary revision arrived at by group-bargaining among themselves.

Citizens dissatisfied with the inequitable results were forced by their interest in the welfare of the schools to participate in an investigation of an adequate salary schedule for New York City teachers. Prior to 1900 teacher salary legislation was characterized by an amazing casualness. In more recent days, other inequitable features of salary legislation resulting in general teacher unrest gave further impetus to the community's cooperation and led directly to the organization in January, 1926, of a Citizens' Committee to investigate teachers' salaries.

SALARY LEGISLATION PRIOR TO 1900

Teachers were conscious of inequalities and inconsistencies in salary schedules for years before the so-called Ahearn Bill of 1898 was drafted. Frequently it took sixteen promotions and twenty years of service for a teacher in the elementary grades to arrive at a salary of $720 a year. Many salary schedules were in effect for the same grade. There was general confusion. The Board of Education attempted to remedy the situation by reducing to fourteen the years of experience required as the qualification for the maximum salary. But even this provision would have put the teacher of the "nineties" only on the salary level of a city street cleaner.

In 1897 the Board of Education finally recommended salary increases. The new schedules became effective - but only on paper; the Board of Estimate and Apportionment refused to appropriate the necessary funds to finance them. Had there been anything but the utmost indiffernce on the public's part, this incongruous situation could not have come about. There followed much talk of reform; more salary schedules were drafted and adopted but the money to make them operative was still not forthcoming.

THE AHEARN BILLS OF 1898 - 1899

Failing repeatedly to get justice from the city authorities, the teachers took their salary problems to Albany. The State Legislature, convinced of the fairness of their case, passed the Ahearn Bill in 1898 providing small salary increases. But again local politicians asserted their authority and prevailed on the Governor to veto the legislation. The year came to a close with the teachers still listening to fair promises and pocketing their grievances.

In the following year, 1899, a second Ahearn Bill was drafted. This legislation succeeded in gaining some public backing and was officially approved by Mayor Van Wyck. It provided minimum salaries for the first, eleventh and sixteenth years of service, leaving to the Board of Education the matter of arranging schedules with graduated increases between the points made mandatory in the bill. It sounded very well - salary campaigners felt encouraged. But, in approving the bill, the Board of Estimate decided to ignore the provisions for yearly increases. Thus, a teacher might teach ten years at the initial salary of $600. before she got an increase of $300. Then she received no more increases until she had served her sixteenth year. Such deliberate evasion of the expressed provisions of the legislation infuriated the teaching body. Public sentiment was aroused. Recognition of this hapless situation in which the teachers found themselves tended to dissipate the apathy which had characterized the public's attitude these many years and we find in the following year, 1900, sufficient community backing for the introduction and passing of the Davis Bill by the State Legislature. This legislation was signed by Governor Roosevelt.

THE DAVIS BILL OF 1900.

Nothing in the history of teacher salary legislation has had a more salutary effect on the entire teaching system than the passage of this Davis Law. Although it continued the older practice of paying higher salaries to men than to women on the theory that supply and demand necessitated such procedure, there were several novel features of the legislation. It established for the first time in New York City a standardization of all salaries. It initiated the present policy of paying definite annual increments. But more important than either of these characteristics was the fact that it provided fairly comfortable incomes for all the city's teachers.

The salaries established by the Davis Bill permitted the city's educators to live on a social and cultural plane much higher, say school administrators, than under the schedules prevailing today. Excellent instructors from all parts of the country were attracted by the generous salaries offered. It is known that many of the city's outstanding educators and administrators came into the system at that time. This era of good salaries and good teachers might have lasted longer had the cost of living remained fairly constant; even had it increased slightly. But unfortunately there set in shortly after the passage of the Davis legislation, a steady increase in the cost of living and a consequent decline in the purchasing power of the dollar. By 1912, the cost of living had leaped ahead some 42 per cent. Teachers' salaries, on the other hand, remained where the Davis Bill of 1900 had put them.

THE EQUAL PAY CAMPAIGN

During these years there were sporadic attempts to remedy the situation but the agitation for equal pay swamped all salary revision based on the existing schedules. This so-called equal pay campaign was waged from 1900 to 1912 and terminated in the passage of the Equal Pay Bill of that date. It was a long and acrimonious fight, its advocates insisting that equal salaries be paid for equal work, regardless of sex. They attacked the Davis Bill. It had established considerably higher salaries for men. The highest pay, for instance, that a woman teacher in the elementary grades could receive was $1,300, whereas a man teaching the same grade might make $2,160 a year.

The equal pay campaigners called upon the administration to eliminate such apparent discriminations and before the state legislature passed the Bill, the Board of Education capitulated. It approved and adopted the theory of equal pay for men and women and in 1912 the state legislature concurred in this adoption by passing the legislation. As the outcome of its enactment little real salary benefit accrued. In fact the equal pay law did not become fully operative for men and women until 1920.

THE GAYNOR COMMISSION

The year 1910 marks a significant out-cropping of real community interest in the problem of adjusting teachers' salaries. It was becoming manifest that efficient public schooling was involved in a fair settlement of the salary situation and this gave rise to the appointment of the so-called Gaynor Commission. This committee, made up of citizens who recognized the need for adequate salaries, carried on an earnest though somewhat superficial investigation. Proceeding on the theory that salaries should be made attractive enough to get and hold men in the profession, the committee proposed that salaries be paid on the basis of the sex of the pupil taught. It recommended, for instance, that teachers of girls in high schools receive a salary of $2500 a year and teachers of boys in high schools $3000 a year, the inference being that men would teach boys and women teach girls. Proponents of equal pay - the campaign was then at its height - were quick to attack the report as violating the principle of equal pay.

The plan recommended by the Gaynor Commission was considered impractical and inexpedient. But in its creation and deliberations is seen a significant contribution. It betokened an awakened and functioning community interest in public education and established the precedent of citizens organizing for the purpose of making an impartial survey of the situation. In recommending salary increases as far back as 1910, it substantiated the teacher's contention of 1919-1920 that there had long been a pressing need for salary adjustment.

LOCKWOOD-DONOHUE BILL OF 1920.

The Equal Pay Bill was followed in the succeeding eight years by minor legislation that sought exemption from its statutes for certain groups of men teachers in the system. Typical of such legislation was the provision, for example, which permitted all men in training schools at the time of its adoption to receive the salary in effect before its passage. (One of the provisions of the Equal Pay Bill had been that no teacher then in the system should suffer salary reduction.)

The next really significant piece of salary legislation, however, was that incorporated in the Lockwood-Donohue Bills of 1919-1920. This legislation, in general, established the salaries that prevail today. The bill was presented by the teachers, passed by the State Legislature and signed by Governor Smith.

As to the actual working out of the provision of the bill, certain conclusions are evident. The increases granted served only to relieve an acute economic situation. In no real sense did they restore to the teacher the full purchasing power of the dollar she got in 1900. Although the new schedules gave the kindergarten to 6B group a relatively larger increase, they did little to relieve the economic burden of high school teachers, principals, and administrators. In fact the Lockwood-Donohue legislation failed to satisfy the needs of the teaching body and became inadequate as a continuing remedy for the situation.

An explanation of this inadequacy may be laid to the fact that, at the time the bill was drafted, experts were of the opinion that a drop in the cost of living was imminent. It was not considered wise, therefore, to grant the teachers' requests in full. This expected decrease did not take place. On the contrary, there had been a slight rise in the prices of essential commodities. Agitation was soon under way for new legislation granting more substantial increases.

The public backing that the teachers were able to enlist in support of this legislation is a far cry from the days of '97. The spirit that animated the Gaynor Commission of 1910 is now in the ascendancy. We find interested citizens willing and eager to appear with the teachers in Albany in support of their plea for salary increases. There has come about in these last fifteen years a fuller realization that in cooperation between parent and teacher, between the public and its schools, there is not only strength but commonsense. The public is beginning to realize that the fundamental basis for paying teachers' salaries should be that which keeps the teacher in condition to render the best service to the community.

If teaching standards were deteriorating, if good instructors were rapidly leaving the system and potentially strong teachers were not entering the system, if it was becoming more and more impossible to attract or retain capable men teachers, then here was a situation to challenge the interest and active participation of all intelligent citizens having at heart the interests of the child and the citizen of tomorrow. Information concerning these facts was derived from a statement issued by the Board of Examiners at this time.

THE RICCA BILL OF 1925-26

By 1924 the teachers' representatives were again in Albany with a measure which attempted to restore, in part, the purchasing power of their dollar. The legislation was introduced into the State Legislature and came to be known as the Ricca Bill. (See Appendix B.)

The story of what happened to this legislation is important since the vicissitudes the teachers experienced in urging its enactment were directly responsible for the creation of the Citizens' Committee on Teachers' Salaries. The State Legislature passed this Ricca Bill in 1925. It was then submitted to Governor Smith, who vetoed the measure on the ground that it was a matter to be settled by the city authorities.

The teachers came back to the city. They appealed to the Board of Education. As a balm of a sort, the Board of Education drew up a bill asking for a lump sum appropriation of approximately $5,700,000 to meet the cost of salary increases. The Board of Estimate threw out the proposal.

THE FRIEDSAM COMMISSION

In the meantime, Governor Smith had appointed a state-wide group of citizens, which became known as the Friedsam Commission, to study the cost of financing education. As a result of its deliberations and conclusions, the so-called Cole-Rice Bill was introduced in the 1926 legislature. If adopted, this legislation would have provided the City of New York with approximately $14,000,000 with which to meet the added expense of teacher salary increases. The Friedsam Commission had no power to investigate the salary situation and salary schedules in the various cities of the State. The teachers, on appealing to it for assistance, were told that such was the case and it was then and there that several members on the Governor's Committee on School Financing conceived the idea of citizens organizing to make a survey of the local salary situation.

Many interested and sympathetic spectators became convinced

that the teachers were getting nowhere with the bills they themselves had drawn up. Their legislation was becoming a political foot-ball and their frequent excursions to the Capitol a matter for facetious comment. Friends of the teachers began to feel that the Albany campaigns had deleterious effects. The continuity of a teacher's classroom work was broken. The emotional stress of a salary campaign engaged in by the city's educators, with its attendant acrimony and ill-feeling, was thought to have an undesirable effect on teaching morale.

The time was ripe for a body of disinterested, non-partisan and impartially-minded citizens to come to the aid of the teachers and the community, to make a thorough and scientific investigation of the whole situation. It was fitting that the suggestion to form such an organization should have come from the United Parents Association of Greater New York Schools. A small group of non-partisan prominent citizens responded immediately to the suggestion made and the machinery for starting such a committee was soon set up. (Detail on the organization of the Committee may be found in Chapter VII).

THE CITIZENS' COMMITTEE ON TEACHERS' SALARIES ORGANIZED

The invitation that this small group of citizens - later to become the Executive Committee of the organization - sent out to representative leaders in industry, business, labor and educational, civic and religious enterprises, read as follows:

> "Let us get at the facts from the point of view of all concerned - the children, the teachers, the Board of Education and the City administration".

This program, in effect, governed the course of the investigation and closely paralleled the Committee's publicity policy. Citizens prominent in all walks of life responded to the call and on January 28, 1926, at the Bar Association Building, these people got together and organized the Citizens' Committee to investigate teachers' salaries. Ralph Jonas, President of the Brooklyn Chamber of Commerce, was elected Chairman and Robert E. Simon, President of the United Parents Association, was appointed chairman of the Executive Committee. Mr. Jonas, however, did not accept and Mr. Simon succeeded him as chairman of the Committee.

Thus, with its organization and personnel completed, the Citizens' Committee set out to learn the facts; to ascertain whether or not the teachers in the public schools were being inadequately paid and if so, how much of an adjustment was necessary to help them meet the increased cost of living. It was in no sense a salary-raising committee. It was thoroughly impartial and had no preconceived ideas. Its five-fold plan of attack on this most fundamental and vital problem, is told in the following pages.

THE SECOND RICCA BILL 1926

Encouraged by the Committee's activities and using its preliminary report, the teachers went back to Albany in 1926 and presented a salary bill which also became known as the Ricca Bill. It was passed by the State Legislature and submitted again to Governor Smith. Before the Governor acted upon it, the Board of Estimate and Apportionment of New

York City petitioned him to veto the Ricca Bill and other teacher salary legislation and submitted a resolution that had been passed which authorized the Mayor and the President of the Board of Education to appoint a committee to study and report on the teacher salary situation. The text of this resolution follows:

> WHEREAS there are pending before the Governor a number of bills passed by the Legislature increasing the salaries of teachers, namely Assembly introductory No. 1238, print No. 1352, by Mr. Ricca; Senate introductory No. 1154, print No. 1984, by Mr. Farrell; Assembly introductory No. 1273, print No. 1394, by Mr. Phelps; Senate print No. 708, by Mr. Antin, and Assembly introductory No. 177, print No. 176, by Mr. Feld; and
>
> WHEREAS the Controller has reported that the bill print No. 1352, Assembly, would require an additional expenditure of $17,000,000 for teachers' salaries next year and that the city is financially unable to meet this increase within the 2 per cent constitutional tax limitation; and
>
> WHEREAS the increases contained in the various bills are not believed to be founded on a scientific or disinterested basis:
>
> THEREFORE be it resolved that a committee of fifteen be designated to make a thorough and scientific study of the entire question of teachers' salaries in the city of New York; five members to be appointed by the President of the Board of Education, ten members to be appointed by the Mayor, and to proceed with diligence and make a report at the earliest possible date; and
>
> Be it further resolved that the secretary of the Board of Estimate and Apportionment transmit a copy of this resolution to the Governor with a request that he withhold this approval from the salary increase bills.

The result of this communication to the Governor was the announcement of his veto, at which time he cited the lack of state funds and the failure of the Legislature to pass the Cole-Rice Bill which would have released money for school financing.

Governor Smith's veto message emphasized the inability to finance the increase within the two per cent taxing limit and pointed out that the Cole Bill increasing state aid would have provided the funds outside of such limitation. The Governor also noted the proposal of the city to name a Commission to study the problem and declared that the Board of Education, not the teachers, should initiate salary legislation. He added that he was satisfied that the city administration "is strongly inclined to do justice to our great army of school teachers".

After this veto, the teachers came back to the city, cooperated with the Citizens' Committee and postponed drafting any more schedules until the official Committee on Teachers' Salaries should be appointed. It was October 11, 1926 before this Committee was appointed by the Mayor and the President of the Board of Education.

The work of this official investigating committee began with conferences with the Citizens' Committee. On three occasions Dr. J. R. McGaughy, Director for the Committee, presented the facts and findings of the Citizens' Committee to this group. Further discussion of the relationship of the Mayor's Committee to the Citizens' Committee and to the city's educators is to be found in the last chapter of this report. (Chapter VII).

In submitting this report, the Citizens' Committee wishes to express its great appreciation for the invaluable cooperation rendered by the Board of Education, the city's teachers, the press and interested and cooperating citizens.

CHAPTER II

PLAN OF ATTACK

The Citizens' Committee studied the problem of teachers' salaries in New York City from five points of view. It was recognized from the very first that no single attack upon the complicated problem could yield all of the facts necessary for a sound solution. The Executive Committee met with the Director and the staff of specialists and decided to approach the problem from the following angles:

First, a comparison of the purchasing power of the present salaries of different groups of teachers in New York City with the purchasing power of the salaries of the groups of teachers in 1910 and in 1900.

Second, a comparison of the increases in teachers' salaries in New York City over a given period with the increases in wages and salaries received by other employed groups during the same length of time.

Third, a comparison of the present salaries paid to New York City teachers with the salaries being paid to corresponding groups of teachers in other large American cities.

Fourth, a study of the adequacy of present salaries in New York City as measured by the economic demands upon these teachers.

Fifth, a study of the degree to which the salaries and teaching conditions in New York City were attracting into the public school system the abler graduates of colleges and teacher training institutions.

In this chapter it is proposed to present a brief summary of the methods of collecting and interpreting the facts discovered by the use of each of the five separate plans of approach to the problem. An attempt will be made to show the bearing of each group of facts upon the final recommendations of the Committee. The detailed computations based on the facts are presented in Chapter V. Completely detailed tabulations of all of the data collected by the Committee will be found in the appendix to this report.

A. THE PURCHASING POWER OF TEACHERS' SALARIES IN 1926

It is an accepted fact that the dollar varies widely from year to year in its purchasing power. The prices of all commodities move up and down under the influence of changing economic conditions. Family income which was sufficient to provide a comfortable living with a few luxuries and with a respectable amount left over for the savings bank in 1910 or in 1913 decreased in its purchasing power until it required the most rigid economy to meet the absolute necessary costs of living in 1920. The same quality and quantity of food which can be bought for $3.00 in one year may require an expenditure of $5.00 or of only $2.50 some other year. It is therefore without meaning or significance to compare the gross number of dollars paid to a teacher in one year with the salary of another year unless this changing purchasing power of the dollar is taken into consideration.

The United States Bureau of Labor Statistics has collected detailed facts concerning the cost of living in the country as a whole and in each of many of the largest American cities since 1913. On the basis of these facts it has published in its bulletins a series of indexes of the cost of living from 1914 until the present date. The total cost of living is divided into six parts, as follows: Food, clothing, housing, fuel and light, house furnishing goods, miscellaneous.

The bulletin of this Bureau issued in February, 1926,* reports that the cost of living in New York City in December, 1925, was 83 per cent higher than was the cost of living in New York City in December, 1914. Expressed in other words, it required $183 in December, 1925, to buy the same quantity and quality of the commodities such as food, rent and clothing which go to make up the total cost of living as could have been bought for $100 in December, 1914. One hundred dollars in 1914 expended upon commodities necessary to living in New York City would go as far as $183 in 1925. Since it required eleven-sixths as many dollars to buy equivalent goods in 1925 each of the 1925 dollars was worth only six-elevenths as much as the 1914 dollar. That is, on a 1914 base the 1925 New York City dollar was worth only 55 cents.

---

*Labor Review, United States Bureau of Labor Statistics, February 1926, Volume XXII, No. 2, page 68.

Prior to 1914 neither the Bureau of Labor Statistics nor any other agency kept records of the changing prices of all the commodities which make up the total cost of living. For many years before that date, however, the Bureau of Labor Statistics published an index which recorded the changing cost of food based on the country as a whole.

In summary, then, the Citizens' Committee had available an index of the total cost of living in New York City from 1914 until December, 1925, and an index of the cost of food for the entire country prior to 1914. In determining the purchasing power of present salaries as compared with those of 1910 or of 1900 the Committee assumed that the cost of living in New York City before 1914 paralleled the changing costs of food in the country as a whole during the given period.

Chart I shows that from 1914 until 1920 the food line and the cost of living line were almost exactly the same. Since the period 1910 to 1915 was unmarked by economic disturbances, there is every reason to believe that there is little error in assuming that the cost of living line followed the cost of food line during these four years.

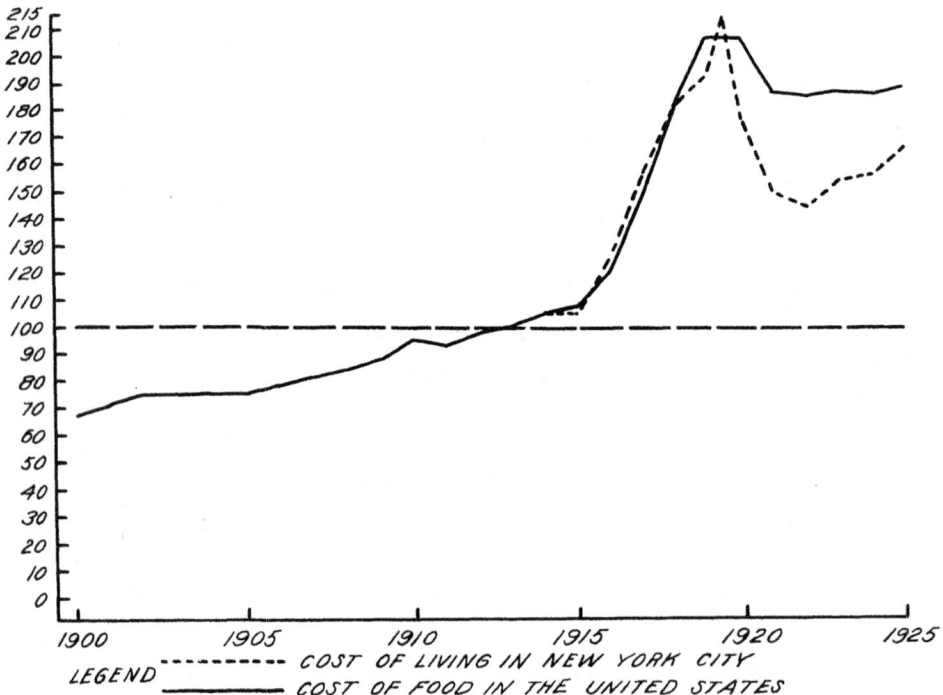

Table I on page 51 of Chapter III shows that it required nearly $202 in December, 1925, to go as far in meeting the cost of living as $100 would have gone in 1910. In other words, the New York City dollar in December, 1925, was worth only 49.6 cents as compared with the 1910 dollar. From 1900 to 1910 the cost of food increased more than one-third; that is, the 1910 dollar was worth only three-fourths as much as the 1900 dollar. On that basis the New York City dollar of December, 1925, would buy less than 37 cents would have bought in 1900.

These facts as summarized above were used by the Committee in comparing the adequacy of present teachers' salaries in New York City with the corresponding salaries paid in 1900 and in 1910. Having determined the relative purchasing power of the teachers' salary dollar at different dates, the Committee proceeded to determine the average salaries paid to the several groups of New York City teachers at present and in 1910. The year 1910 was chosen as a date of reference because it was preceded by a period free from economic disturbances of any unusual sort and because it was unaffected by the unrest and fluctuations which immediately preceded the outbreak of the Great War.

The average salaries of each group of teachers in 1910 and in 1926 were determined from computations based on the published figures in the Budget Estimates of the Board of Education for these two years. These printed reports give complete details concerning the number of men and women teachers and the salaries paid to them.

In 1926 there were 178 distinct groups whose salaries were paid from the general school fund. In 1910 there were only 103 groups specified in the Budget Estimate. The Committee combined these detailed schedules so that they would show the facts for groups such as kindergarten to grade 6B teachers, teachers in junior high school and in grades seven to nine, teachers in senior high schools, principals of elementary schools, and the other groups of administrative and supervisory officers to be found in the New York City schools.

From this analysis of the Budget Estimates of the Board of Education such facts as these were made available: There were 366 men teaching in the grades from kindergarten to 6B in 1910; their average salary was $1,318. In 1925 there were 409 men teaching in these same grades at an average salary of $1,818. In 1910 there were 10,982 women teaching in the grades from kindergarten to 6B at an average salary of $913. In 1925 14,030 women were teaching in these grades at an average salary of $2,451.

These two sets of facts were then put together in order to determine the purchasing power of present salaries in comparison with that of 1910 salaries. To illustrate, the average salary of $2,451 received by women elementary teachers in 1926 is equivalent to $1,215 of 1910 money since the present dollar will purchase only as much as 49.6 cents would purchase in 1910. The average salary actually received by women elementary teachers in 1910 was $931; $1,215 is 133 per cent of $931, therefore the present purchasing power of the average salary of women elementary teachers is 33 per cent greater than that of the average salary of 1910.

The records of the Board of Education do not give summaries of the salaries paid to different teacher groups in 1900. Instead, the records show the salary paid to each individual teacher in each separate school building. To compute the average salary paid to any one group of teachers would require an enormous amount of clerical and statistical work. Between 1900 and 1910 there was no change in salary schedules in New York City. If the same proportion of teachers were teaching at each level of the salary schedules in these two years, the average salaries paid in 1900 would be exactly equal to those paid in 1910. The Committee accepted this assumption as reasonable and related the purchasing power of present average salaries to that of the salaries of 1900. Since the cost of food increased one-third from 1900 to 1910, the purchasing power of present salaries on the 1900 base is only three-fourths as great as the present purchasing power figured on the 1910 base.

The women elementary teachers will serve as an illustration. The average salary of this group in 1910 was $931, as stated above. If the same proportion of the group were teaching their first year, their second year and so on throughout the schedule as was the case for this group in 1910, the average salary of this group was $931 in 1900 also. The dollar of 1926 would purchase only as much as 36.6 cents would purchase in 1900. Therefore the average salary of $2,451 in 1926 was equivalent to only 98 per cent as much as the average salary of $931 in 1900.

Since computing the purchasing power of present salaries on the 1900 base involves two assumptions, neither of which can be proved - (1) that the teaching groups were distributed over the different years of the salary schedule in 1900 somewhat as they were in 1910, and (2) that the cost of living line paralleled the cost of food line during this same period (See Chart I, page 24) - the Committee has attached little importance to its computations of the purchasing power of present salaries on the 1900 base.

Some of the outstanding facts discovered in this study are reported in Section A of Chapter III. Detailed statistical tables resulting from this study are presented in Appendix A, pp. 224 - 229.

B. TEACHER SALARY INCREASES COMPARED WITH INCREASES OF OTHER WAGES AND SALARIES

Many economic and industrial agencies have collected and published facts concerning the trend in the wages and salaries of several groups of employees in public and private institutions. The Committee made a study of these facts as published in order to determine whether the salaries of New York City teachers have been increased more or less rapidly than have the wages and salaries of other groups.

This relationship is discussed in Section B of Chapter III, and detailed statistical tables and charts are presented in Appendix A, page 223. In general, wages and salaries in private or commercial enterprises have increased more rapidly and the salaries of other public employees have increased less rapidly than have the salaries of New

York City teachers in the last ten or fifteen years.

C. TEACHERS' SALARIES IN NEW YORK CITY AND IN OTHER LARGE AMERICAN CITIES

Every city and hamlet in the United States has met and solved in some way the problem of determining how much it shall pay to public school teachers. It was the Committee's belief that a careful study of the salary situations in a few of the largest cities would be of value in assisting it to reach valid conclusions concerning the New York City problem. The Director of this study visited eight such cities and made a personal study of the amounts paid to each group of teachers, of the basis upon which salaries were determined, of the relationship between the salaries of different groups of teachers within the same city and of the proportion of men and women teachers in each teacher group in each city.

The facts thus secured were tabulated and studied, especially with reference to the relationships between the average salaries paid to different groups such as elementary and senior high school teachers, or teachers and principals of the same types of schools in each city. This part of the study served as a valuable check on the relationships between the schedules proposed for the different teaching, supervisory, and administrative groups in New York City.

Practically every group of employees of these city boards of education is receiving a smaller salary than the corresponding group in New York City. There are no facts available concerning the relative cost of living in American cities. It was therefore impossible for the Committee to determine whether the purchasing power of teachers' salaries in other cities is greater or less than in New York City.

The summary of the facts determined by this study will be found in Section 3 of Chapter III, and detailed statistical tables are presented in Appendix A, pp. 230 - 232.

D. ECONOMIC AND PROFESSIONAL STATUS OF NEW YORK CITY TEACHERS

Early in its work the Citizens' Committee discovered that there were many significant facts concerning the teachers of New York City which were not available in the records of the Board of Education. The statistics which were available could not be interpreted to show the kind and amount of professional preparation which had been secured by the teachers of the system. Neither would these records show anything concerning the economic status of teachers - how much of their salaries they were expending for such necessities as rent, food and clothing, or the amount of their earnings during the regular school year and during the summer vacation in addition to their regular salaries from the Board of Education.

The Committee was therefore forced to the decision that it had to secure the cooperation of the individual teachers in reporting such facts as were essential to a scientific determination of fair and equitable adjustments in salary schedules. This feature of the Committee's work was by far the most important of the investigations undertaken and required heavy expenditure of time and money.

In order that these significant facts might be secured by the Committee a voluntary confidential inquiry blank was drawn up and printed. Each teacher received two copies, one of which was marked "duplicate" and was to be used by the teacher for study and to guide her in preparing in advance the information which was to be copied on the other blank which was returned to the Committee. More than 60,000 of these blanks were printed - about 30,000 duplicate copies and about 30,000 to be used for the final report. A sufficient number of each type of blank for all of the teachers and administrative and supervisory officers in each school building was tied up in a package and delivered to the principal's office by a large distributing company which was given the contract to distribute the blanks and to collect them and return them to the Committee's office.

Chart II is a reproduction of the duplicate form of the blank and Chart III of one of the reports actually filled out and returned to the Committee. This latter blank had a serial number on the title page and the same serial number on a perforated slip at the bottom of the last page. On this slip were blanks to be filled out with the teacher's name and address. Each teacher also was supplied with two envelopes. On a fixed day all of the teachers filled out the second blank, tore off the perforated slip bearing her name, placed the report in one envelope and the detached slip in another, sealed the envelopes and returned them to the principal's office. The principal tied them up into a package ready for collection.

CHART II. REPRODUCTION OF COPY OF INQUIRY BLANK

VOLUNTARY CONFIDENTIAL REPORT
to the
Citizens Committee on Teachers Salaries

EXECUTIVE COMMITTEE

Robert E. Simon, President of the United Parents Association, Chairman.
Mrs. H. Edward Dreier, President of the Women's City Club; First Vice-president.
Mrs. Seymour Barnard, President of the Parents League of Brooklyn.
Miss Martha Draper, Vice-President of Public Education Association.
E. W. Edwards, Chairman of the Committee of Education of the New York State Federation of Labor.
Dr. John H. Finley, Chairman of the Educational Committees of the New York State Chamber of Commerce and of the Merchants Association.
Dr. Lee K. Frankel, Vice-President of the Metropolitan Life Insurance Company.
Raymond V. Ingersoll, Impartial Chairman of the cloak, suit and skirt industries.

Frederick H. Ecker, President of the New York State Chamber of Commerce; Second Vice-president.
Joseph P. Cotton, President of the Public Education Association; Third Vice-president.
Ex-Senator Charles C. Lockwood.
John Martin, Ex-Member of New York City Board of Education.
Mrs. Henry Moskowitz, Member of Board of Directors, Women's City Club.
Mrs. George V. Mullan, Former member of the Board of Education.
Lawson Purdy, Secretary of the Charity Organization Society.
Nelson S. Spencer, Former President of the Men's City Club.
Mrs. Joseph Swan, Trustee of Teachers College, Columbia University.

ADVISORY COMMITTEE

Donald R. Belcher, Statistician, American Telephone & Telegraph Company.
Dr. Louis I. Dublin, Statistician, Metropolitan Life Insurance Company.

Prof. Willford I. King, Economist, National Bureau of Economic Research, Inc.
Dr. Albert Shiels, Teachers College, Columbia University.

FOREWORD

The Citizens Committee on Teachers Salaries recognizes the major importance of the teacher's work and seeks a just and adequate compensation, commensurate with the value of the teacher's services. It believes that an impartial, comprehensive survey of existing conditions, made by experts of the highest authority under the auspices of, and presented by a group of disinterested citizens, will command the attention and respect of the community and should prove a contribution to the teachers, to the citizens and to the children of the City.

The selection of Dr. J. R. McGaughy of Teachers College, a national authority on school finance, to act as director of the survey was approved by the Advisory Committee of experts and his preliminary report on teachers salaries was indorsed by them. This report was also indorsed by William R. Lasher, Chairman of the Joint Salary Committee, who characterized the analysis of teachers salaries in relation to the cost of living as the best and most effective he had seen.

The result of this preliminary report, showing as it did the need for salary adjustments, made it obligatory for the Citizens Committee to go futher if it was to accomplish the purpose for which it was organized. Hence this voluntary Inquiry Blank which, in the opinion of experts, is a desirable procedure for gaining such information as will insure constructive, impartial conclusions. Obviously the experience of an individual or the experiens of a group of individuals is valueless; sound conclusions can be based only on facts—facts that show exactly how economic conditions affect large groups and to what extent they are affected.

The recommendations which the experts make, if they are to be sound—if they are to be taken seriously by the tax-paying public and by legislative bodies—must of necessity be based on facts. By answering fully and accurately all the questions, you will be making it possible for the Committee to present authoritative recommendations. Although filling out the report is entirely voluntary on your part, we trust you will appreciate the importance of getting a response from every one in the educational system.

In submitting this blank to you, the Citizens Committee has the approval and indorsement of President Ryan and the Administrative Staff of the Board of Education and the support of the teachers organizations.

N? 16516 A

May, 1926
NEW YORK CITY

CONFIDENTIAL REPORT
TO THE
CITIZENS COMMITTEE ON TEACHERS SALARIES

You are invited to fill out carefully the following report. This report will be treated as confidential in every particular. The reason for your signature is obvious—recommendations based on anonymous returns would be unconvincing and worthless. Sign your name on the blank line indicated; tear off on perforated line and enclose the slip in the envelope which accompanies this blank. Thus, your name will not appear on the report when it is received for tabulation by the clerical staff *nor will it ever be used in any connection other than for the purpose of the committee's confidential inquiry.*

J. R. McGaughy, *Director.*

A. *Personal Data.*
1. Designate sex with check mark: Man ✓   Woman ____
2. What is your residence address? 262 N. Oak Ave, Ridgefield, N.J. Apartment number? House
3. What is your position in the school system? Assistant teacher ____ If a teacher, what grade or subjects do you teach? Physics — Chemistry
4. What was the date of your first appointment in the New York City public school system? Oct. 1904

B. *Teaching Experience.*
5. Fill in the form below to show what your teaching experience has been:

Dates	Name of City	Name or Number of School	Grades or subjects taught or Educational Position Held
Feb–June '04	N.Y.	85 B'klyn	2B–8B Public Jr
Oct. 1904 to Oct. 1914	N.Y.	145 "	Major Eng. + Amer. Hist. Civics Minor P.T. Nat. Sci.
Oct. 1914 to date	N.Y.	W.I. H.S.	Physics, Chem. History

C. *Salary Data.*
6. Fill in the blanks below to indicate the sources and amounts of your *earned income* for the year beginning April 1st, 1925 and ending March 31st, 1926.

Sources of Earned Income:	Amount received during regular school year:	Amount received during summer vacation:
a. From Board of Education:		
(1) Salary for day school	$ 3700	$
(2) Salary for evening school	$	$
(3) Salary for other work for Board of Education	$	$
b. Earnings from sources other than Board of Education. (Include *earnings* only and not the income from interest, rents, royalties, annuities, life insurance, etc.) Specify how you earned this additional income on blank lines below:		
(1)	$ none	$
(2)	$	$
(3)	$	$
(4)	$	$
(5)	$	$

7. What is the maximum salary for your group under the present salary schedule? __3700__
8. If you are receiving the maximum salary for your group, in what year did you qualify for it? __1918__
   If you are not receiving the maximum, in what year will you qualify for it? _____
9. What was your annual salary the first year you taught as a regular full-time teacher in the New York City public schools? $ __900__
10. If you were teaching as a regular full-time teacher before entering the New York City public school system, what was your annual salary for the last year of that service? $ _____

D. *Educational Preparation.*
11. Fill in the blanks below to show what has been your educational preparation beyond the elementary school grades:

Type of Institution	Name of Institution	No. of regular academic years attended.*	Summer Session Attendance		Names of Diplomas or Degrees received
			No. of Sessions	Total No. of Weeks	
High School (Secondary)	Boys H.S. Bklyn	4	—	—	Diploma
Normal School or Teachers College (Teacher Training)	Bklyn Trg. Trng. School	2	—	—	Diploma
College or University (Undergraduate)	NYU	3	—	—	B.S.
College or University (Post-graduate)	NYU	1	not yet written master's thesis		

   * Report part-time attendance during regular academic year, and extramural and extension course attendance, as fractional parts of a regular year. Thus, a 30 hour course is 1/10 of a college year.

E. *Teaching Certification.*
12. Under what license are you now teaching? __Chem. — assistant__
13. On what date did you begin teaching under this license? __1914 Oct.__
14. Have you taught under other New York City licenses? __yes — Licenses 4A   6B__
    If so, name them here: __Promotion 7A-8A Graduating Class 8B__
    __Promotion License Sci. & Geog.   Physics H.S. assistant__

15. Have you qualified for a license of higher grade than the one you are now using? _____
    If so, what is your rating on the waiting list? _____

F. *Cost of Living Data.*
   (Certain questions are here asked in order to secure a more adequate picture of the economic status of New York City teachers. It is not to be inferred that recommendations as to salary schedules are to be based upon the data obtained.)

   Answer the questions of No. 16, No. 17, or No. 18 below. Do not answer more than *one* of the three.

16. If you are married and are living with wife (or husband) answer these questions:
    a. How many children have you? __1__
    b. How many persons, not including yourself, are chiefly dependent on your income? __3__
    c. What is the annual rental (or rental value if you own your own home) of the apartment or house in which you live? $__1800__ If rented, does the landlord supply furnishings? __No__ Heat? __no__ Janitor service? __No__
       How many rooms has it? __6__ How many of these rooms do you sub-rent? __0__
       Do you sub-rent the rooms furnished or unfurnished? _____
       What is the annual rental derived from all these sub-rented rooms combined? $__0__ Do the rentals here reported include heat and janitor service? _____
    d. What is your monthly expense for meals? $__?__
    e. What was your total expense on account of summer school attendance in 1923? — $_____
       In 1924? — $_____ In 1925? — $_____

17. If you do not come under the classification of No. 16 above but are living at home as one of a family of near relatives, answer these questions:
    a. How many persons, not including yourself, are there in the family? _____
    b. How many persons are chiefly dependent on your income? _____
    c. If you pay a definite amount as room rent, what is the amount per month? $_____
    d. What is your monthly expense for meals? $_____
    e. What was your total expense on account of summer school attendance in 1923? $_____
       In 1924? $_____ In 1925? $_____

18. If you do not come under the classification of either No. 16 or No. 17, answer these questions:
    a. How many persons are chiefly dependent on your income? _____
    b. What is the annual rental which you pay (or rental value if you own your own home) for your share of the room, apartment or house in which you live? $_____ Is it rented furnished or unfurnished? _____ How much do you receive annually from sub-rented rooms? $_____
       Do you sub-rent the rooms furnished or unfurnished? _____ Do the rentals here reported include heat and janitor service? _____
    c. What is your monthly expense for meals? — $_____
    d. What was your total expense on account of summer school attendance in 1923? — $_____
       In 1924? — $_____ In 1925? — $_____

CHART III. REPRODUCTION OF DUPLICATE COPY OF INQUIRY BLANK

DUPLICATE COPY — This is a duplicate or sample copy of the Voluntary Confidential Inquiry Blank. It is exactly the same as the blank which you will fill out later. The purpose of placing it in your hands in advance is that you may familiarize yourself with the nature of the questions to be asked.

VOLUNTARY CONFIDENTIAL REPORT
to the
Citizens Committee on Teachers Salaries

EXECUTIVE COMMITTEE

Robert E. Simon, President of the United Parents Association, Chairman.
Mrs. H. Edward Dreier, President of the Women's City Club; First Vice-president.
Mrs. Seymour Barnard, President of the Parents League of Brooklyn.
Miss Martha Draper, Vice-President of Public Education Association.
E. W. Edwards, Chairman of the Committee of Education of the New York State Federation of Labor.
Dr. John H. Finley, Chairman of the Educational Committees of the New York State Chamber of Commerce and of the Merchants Association.
Dr. Lee K. Frankel, Vice-President of the Metropolitan Life Insurance Company.
Raymond V. Ingersoll, Impartial Chairman of the cloak, suit and skirt industries.

Frederick H. Ecker, President of the New York State Chamber of Commerce; Second Vice-president.
Joseph P. Cotton, President of the Public Education Association; Third Vice-president.
Ex-Senator Charles C. Lockwood.
John Martin, Ex-Member of New York City Board of Education.
Mrs. Henry Moskowitz, Member of Board of Directors, Women's City Club.
Mrs. George V. Mullan, Former member of the Board of Education.
Lawson Purdy, Secretary of the Charity Organization Soci.y.
Nelson S. Spencer, Former President of the Men's City Club.
Mrs. Joseph Swan, Trustee of Teachers College, Columbia University.

ADVISORY COMMITTEE

Donald R. Belcher, Statistician, American Telephone & Telegraph Company.
Dr. Louis I. Dublin, Statistician, Metropolitan Life Insurance Company.

Prof. Willford I. King, Economist, National Bureau of Economic Research, Inc.
Dr. Albert Shiels, Teachers College, Columbia University.

FOREWORD

The Citizens Committee on Teachers Salaries recognizes the major importance of the teacher's work and seeks a just and adequate compensation, commensurate with the value of the teacher's services. It believes that an impartial, comprehensive survey of existing conditions, made by experts of the highest authority under the auspices of, and presented by a group of disinterested citizens, will command the attention and respect of the community and should prove a contribution to the teachers, to the citizens and to the children of the City.

The selection of Dr. J. R. McGaughy of Teachers College, a national authority on school finance, to act as director of the survey was approved by the Advisory Committee of experts and his preliminary report on teachers salaries was indorsed by them. This report was also indorsed by William R. Lasher, Chairman of the Joint Salary Committee, who characterized the analysis of teachers salaries in relation to the cost of living as the best and most effective he had seen.

The result of this preliminary report, showing as it did the need for salary adjustments, made it obligatory for the Citizens Committee to go futher if it was to accomplish the purpos for which it was organized. Hence this voluntary Inquiry Blank which, in the opinion of experts, is a desirable procedure for gaining such information as will insure constructive, impartial conclusions. Obviously the experience of an individual or the experienes of a group of individuals is valueless; sound conclusions can be based only on facts—facts that show exactly how economic conditions affect large groups and to what extent they are affected.

The recommendations which the experts make, if they are to be sound—if they are to be taken seriously by the tax-paying public and by legislative bodies—must of necessity be based on facts. By answering fully and accura:ely all the questions, you will be making it possible for the Committee to present authoritative recommendations. Although filling out the report is entirely voluntary on your part, we trust you will appreciate the importance of getting a response from every one in the educational system.

In submitting this blank to you, the Citizens Committee has the approval and indorsement of President Ryan and the Administrative Staff of the Board of Education and the support of the teachers organizations.

May, 1926
NEW YORK CITY

CHART II (continued)

DUPLICATE COPY

CONFIDENTIAL REPORT
TO THE
CITIZENS COMMITTEE ON TEACHERS SALARIES

You are invited to fill out carefully the following report. This report will be treated as confidential in every particular. The reason for your signature is obvious—recommendations based on anonymous returns would be unconvincing and worthless. Sign your name on the blank line indicated; tear off on perforated line and enclose the slip in the envelope which accompanies this blank. Thus, your name will not appear on the report when it is received for tabulation by the clerical staff *nor will it ever be used in any connection other than for the purpose of the committee's confidential inquiry.*

J. R. McGAUGHY, *Director.*

A. *Personal Data.*
1. Designate sex with check mark: Man_____ Woman_____
2. What is your residence address? _____ Apartment number? _____
3. What is your position in the school system? _____ If a teacher, what grade or subjects do you teach? _____
4. What was the date of your first appointment in the New York City public school system? _____

B. *Teaching Experience.*
5. Fill in the form below to show what your teaching experience has been:

Dates	Name of City	Name or Number of School	Grades or subjects taught or Educational Position Held

C. *Salary Data.*
6. Fill in the blanks below to indicate the sources and amounts of your *earned income* for the year beginning April 1st, 1925 and ending March 31st, 1926.

Sources of Earned Income:	Amount received during regular school year:	Amount received during summer vacation:
a. From Board of Education:		
(1) Salary for day school _____	$ _____	$ _____
(2) Salary for evening school _____	$ _____	$ _____
(3) Salary for other work for Board of Education	$ _____	$ _____
b. Earnings from sources other than Board of Education. (Include *earnings* only and not the income from interest, rents, royalties, annuities, life insurance, etc.) Specify how you earned this additional income on blank lines below:		
(1) _____	$ _____	$ _____
(2) _____	$ _____	$ _____
(3) _____	$ _____	$ _____
(4) _____	$ _____	$ _____
(5) _____	$ _____	$ _____

DUPLICATE COPY   **CHART II (continued)**

7. What is the maximum salary for your group under the present salary schedule? _____
8. If you are receiving the maximum salary for your group, in what year did you qualify for it? _____
   If you are not receiving the maximum, in what year will you qualify for it? _____
9. What was your annual salary the first year you taught as a regular full-time teacher in the New York City public schools? $_____
10. If you were teaching as a regular full-time teacher before entering the New York City public school system, what was your annual salary for the last year of that service? $_____

D. *Educational Preparation.*
11. Fill in the blanks below to show what has been your educational preparation beyond the elementary school grades:

Type of Institution	Name of Institution	No. of regular academic years attended.*	Summer Session Attendance		Names of Diplomas or Degrees received
			No. of Sessions	Total No. of Weeks	
High School (Secondary)					
Normal School or Teachers College (Teacher Training)					
College or University (Undergraduate)					
College or University (Post-graduate)					

* Report part-time attendance during regular academic year, and extramural and extension course attendance, as fractional parts of a regular year. Thus, a 30 hour course is 1/10 of a college year.

E. *Teaching Certification.*
12. Under what license are you now teaching? _____
13. On what date did you begin teaching under this license? _____
14. Have you taught under other New York City licenses? _____
    If so, name them here: _____

___

This will be a detachable slip for your name and number of your school.

DUPLICATE COPY

CHART II (continued)

15. Have you qualified for a license of higher grade than the one you are now using? _____
    If so, what is your rating on the waiting list? _____

F. *Cost of Living Data.*
   (Certain questions are here asked in order to secure a more adequate picture of the economic status of New York City teachers. It is not to be inferred that recommendations as to salary schedules are to be based upon the data obtained.)
   Answer the questions of No. 16, No. 17, or No. 18 below. Do not answer more than *one* of the three.

16. If you are married and are living with wife (or husband) answer these questions:
    a. How many children have you? _____
    b. How many persons, not including yourself, are chiefly dependent on your income? _____
    c. What is the annual rental (or rental value if you own your own home) of the apartment or house in which you live? $_____ If rented, does the landlord supply furnishings?_____ Heat?_____
       Janitor service? _____
       How many rooms has it? _____ How many of these rooms do you sub-rent? _____
       Do you sub-rent the rooms furnished or unfurnished? _____
       What is the annual rental derived from all these sub-rented rooms combined? $_____ Do the rentals here reported include heat and janitor service? _____
    d. What is your monthly expense for meals? $_____
    e. What was your total expense on account of summer school attendance in 1923? — $_____
       In 1924? — $_____ In 1925? — $_____

17. If you do not come under the classification of No. 16 above but are living at home as one of a family of near relatives, answer these questions:
    a. How many persons, not including yourself, are there in the family? _____
    b. How many persons are chiefly dependent on your income? _____
    c. If you pay a definite amount as room rent, what is the amount per month? $_____
    d. What is your monthly expense for meals? $_____
    e. What was your total expense on account of summer school attendance in 1923? $_____
       In 1924? $_____ In 1925? $_____

18. If you do not come under the classification of either No. 16 or No. 17, answer these questions:
    a. How many persons are chiefly dependent on your income? _____
    b. What is the annual rental which you pay (or rental value if you own your own home) for your share of the room, apartment or house in which you live? $_____ Is it rented furnished or unfurnished? _____ How much do you receive annually from sub-rented rooms? $_____
       Do you sub-rent the rooms furnished or unfurnished? _____ Do the rentals here reported include heat and janitor service? _____
    c. What is your monthly expense for meals? — $_____
    d. What was your total expense on account of summer school attendance in 1923? — $_____
       In 1924? — $_____ In 1925? — $_____

The Committee was unwilling to base its study on anonymous reports by teachers. The perforated slip with the serial number made it impossible for those who tabulated the data from the reports to associate any teacher's name with the facts reported and yet enabled the Committee to verify any figures which seemed inaccurate.

The superintendent of schools sent out a form letter to be posted on a bulletin board in each building. This letter urged the cooperation of the teachers with the Citizens' Committee, but stated emphatically that the whole matter was to be entirely voluntary on the part of each teacher. It is a very interesting fact that many teachers who did not care to cooperate with the Committee were unwilling to make this fact known to their principals. As a result, 5,000 reports properly sealed up in the envelopes provided were returned to the Committee entirely blank. A total of 11,081 were filled out by the teachers and became the basis of the Committee's study.

Approximately one-third of the women teachers and two-thirds of the men teachers returned the blanks properly filled out with the facts sought by the Committee. There was a higher percentage of returns from the high school teachers than from the elementary teachers. The Committee was at once faced by the necessity of determining whether the women teachers who filled out the reports were a fair statistical sampling of the whole group of women teachers in the school system. This phase of the investigation convinced the Committee that those women who had cooperated in the study were in no particular different from the total group of women teachers.

The facts for the women who filled out the blanks were compared with all available facts for all women teachers. For instance, the average salary reported by the elementary women teachers was $2,475, while the average salary for all the women elementary teachers in New York City was $2,451. The average salary reported by women teachers in the junior high school and in grades seven, eight and nine was $3,140; that of the total group of women teaching in these grades was $3,120. Of the woman senior high school teachers who reported 41 per cent were receiving the maximum salary for high school teachers. In the whole senior high school group 44 per cent of the women teachers were receiving the maximum salary. Fifty-three per cent of the kindergarten teachers who replied were receiving the maximum salary while 54 per cent of all kindergarten teachers were found to be at the maximum for their schedule. Such comparisons as these convinced the Committee that it was an entirely safe statistical procedure to assume that the facts reported by those who filled out the voluntary inquiry blanks might be accepted as true of all the teachers in the school system.

The Committee's tabulation and interpretation of the 11,000 individual reports was a prodigious task. Each report was gone over carefully by students in post-graduate courses in education and the facts there reported were copied in code in the margins of the report ready to be transferred to Hollerith cards. After each return had been coded and the coding checked as to its accuracy, the inquiry blanks were turned over to the Metropolitan Life Insurance Company. This company donated the services of its entire mechanical tabulation department in punching an original white and a duplicate pink Hollerith card for each teacher's report and in running these 11,000 cards some thousands of times through Powers electrical sorting machines to build up detailed statistical tables summarizing all of the facts reported by each group of teachers in the whole school system. It is estimated that the opening of envelopes and the coding and punching and tabulating which were necessary required more than 600,000 separate operations. The statistical tables made by the Metropolitan Life Insurance Company were then turned over to experienced statisticians who performed the computations necessary to an interpretation of the great mass of facts which had been collected.

The questions of the inquiry blank were arranged so that they divided all teachers into three economic groups. One section was to be filled out only by those who were married and were living with husband or wife. A second group of questions was to be answered by those who were not married, but were living at home - for instance, with parents or with married brothers or sisters. The third group of questions was to be answered only by those who did not belong in either of the first two groups, that is, by those who were unmarried persons living away from home. Since all persons were also required to state whether they were man or woman, the Committee had available certain economic facts for each of six distinct groups - men teachers living under each of these three conditions and likewise the three groups of women teachers. In tabulating all of the facts from the questionnaire each professional group, such as elementary teachers or high school principals, was broken up into these six classifications, making it possible to determine how each economic group compared with every other in such matters as length of teaching experience, amount of professional preparation and annual expenses for food or for rent.

Early in its deliberations the Committee decided to use the two big constant items of food and rent as an index of the cost of living requirements of the New York City teachers. In so doing it had two considerations in mind. In the first place, to have requested detailed information concerning a teacher's expenses for all items of her budget would have added greatly to the length and complexity of the report. This would have increased very much the cost of tabulation and interpretation and would undoubtedly have dissuaded many teachers from attempting to fill out the inquiry blank. In the second place, it seemed reasonable to assume that the large majority of teachers do not keep a carefully itemized distribution of expenses. To ask such teachers to report expenses other than for the larger items of food and rent would have resulted in wholesale guessing and inaccuracy.

A number of studies of the budgets of teachers had already been made. These studies were in close agreement that the typical teacher spends from 45 to 50 per cent of her total income for food and rent. The outstanding studies of this sort were state-wide investigations in Michigan and California. A study of the expense budgets of teachers in New York State *, completed after the Committee had reached its decision, indicates that the two items of food and rent constituted almost a perfect index of the teacher's total living expense. This study offered convincing evidence that the Committee's original decision was sound and wise.

The questions of the inquiry blank with relation to the expenses for food and for rent were stated in such detail as to give the most significant facts which would have a bearing upon the true economic status of the teacher. Each teacher, for instance, reported the number of rooms rented, the total annual rent paid out, the number of these rooms which were sub-rented to others and the annual income from such sub-rentals, and a statement as to whether the rooms were rented furnished or unfurnished and whether heat and janitor service were supplied.

The Committee did not attempt to make a separate study of the number and cost of meals prepared at home and of those purchased at restaurants or boarding houses. The one question asked concerning food was - "What is your monthly expense for meals?". Married teachers were also asked to report the number of children in the family, and all teachers were required to state "The number of persons chiefly dependent upon their income".

---

*The Influence of Variations in Cost of Living of Teachers on Educational Needs, David P. Harry. To be published by the Bureau of Publications, Teachers College, Columbia University, New York City.

E. ATTRACTIVENESS OF NEW YORK CITY SALARIES TO OUTSIDE TEACHERS

The fifth plan of attack upon the salary problem in New York City was an attempt to determine the degree to which teacher salaries now paid in New York City were serving to attract outside teachers into the local school system. One item of the voluntary inquiry blank mentioned above had a direct bearing upon this question - each teacher was asked to report the number of years which she had taught outside the public schools of New York City. From the answers to this question it was possible to determine the percentage of each teaching group which had been drawn from the experienced teachers of other school systems. To supplement this information the Committee sent a letter to many normal schools and to colleges and universities of the eastern United States which maintain teacher training departments. This letter requested information as to the percentage of their graduates who entered the New York City schools and the degree to which these graduates considered such educational positions to be desirable.

There was a good percentage of replies to this letter from the heads of such teacher training institutions, but no attempt was made to interpret these replies statistically. It was discovered that a very small percentage of the graduates of such institutions were entering the public schools of New York City. The reason most commonly given, however, was not that the salaries were too low to be attractive, but that the Board of Education's regulations governing entrance were such that they dissuaded any large number from attempting to secure appointment.

This chapter of the report has given in detail the five-fold plan of attack adopted by the Citizens' Committee on Teachers' Salaries in attempting to reach sound recommendations concerning a fair and equitable adjustment of teachers' salaries in New York City. Undoubtedly the Committee could have approached its problem by using another or additional procedures. One of the most obvious and valuable of these plans would have been a detailed study of the corresponding expenditures of teachers in other cities for food and rent. As is stated earlier in this chapter, the Bureau of Labor Statistics does not have available figures on the relative cost of living in American cities. Such a study by the Committee would have required an enormous expenditure of time and money, however, and the Committee considered it unwise to attempt it. All of the other facts which the Committee needed for its guidance were found to be available as a result of some one of the five separate studies which it made.

CHAPTER III

THE FACTS DISCOVERED

In the preceding chapter the five plans of attacking the teacher salary problem have been outlined and explained. Particular emphasis has been given to the methods of collecting and interpreting these facts. In the present chapter it is proposed to present to the reader a summary of the facts which were discovered in each of the five studies which were made by the Committee.

It is not proposed to present in this chapter a greatly detailed exposition of these facts. It is probably true that only a small percentage of those who read this report would be interested in such an exhaustive analysis. Any person who has need for such detailed facts, or who cares to verify the statements made in this chapter, will find the detailed statistical tables which are the bases of this discussion in Appendix A at the end of this report.

It is not claimed that all of the facts presented in this chapter have had a direct bearing upon the recommendations as to salary schedules. Some of the facts here presented, in particular some of those which were derived from the 11,000 inquiry blanks filled out by teachers, are presented for the sole reason that they are of interest from a social or professional point of view. So far as the Committee is able to discover, detailed data concerning the economic status of so large a number of teachers has never before been collected and it has accepted the responsibility of making these facts available, even though they were not of direct and immediate significance in affecting the Committee's recommendations.

The facts discovered in each of the five separate studies undertaken by the Committee will be presented in separate sections of this chapter. The first section presents the data concerning the purchasing power of present salaries of teachers as compared with the salaries of corresponding groups in 1910 and in 1900.

A. RELATIVE PURCHASING POWER OF 1926 SALARIES

In the preceding chapter has been given a complete explanation of the method of computing the index of the cost of living which was accepted by the Citizens' Committee. Table III in Appendix A, page 224 gives the detail of the fluctuations in the cost of living in New York City from December 1914 to December 1925.

This table shows that the cost of food in 1919 was 91 per cent higher than in 1914, that it reached a low point only 50 per cent higher than in 1914 in December, 1922, and that it rose again to a point 63 per cent above the 1914 cost in December, 1925.

In like manner five other items of the cost of living are traced through their rise and fall in New York City throughout this eleven-year period. Clothing cost more than three times as much in 1919 and 1920 as it did in 1914 and then prices receded until the cost was a little less than twice as high in December, 1925, as it had been in 1914.

The cost of rent and of fuel and light have followed a very different line than have the other items of expenditure in New York City during these eleven years. Table III of the Appendix shows that these increases have been quite steadily upward throughout the whole eleven years instead of rising to a high peak at about 1920 and settling back somewhat before 1926. In December, 1925, it required two and a half times as much money as in 1914 to buy a given amount of fuel and light.

This table shows that when these six items of the cost of living - food, clothing, housing, fuel and light, house furnishing goods and miscellaneous - are combined into the total cost of living in New York City, the necessary expenditure in December, 1925, was 83 per cent higher than in December, 1914. As in the case of the separate items of food and clothing, the total cost of living reached a high peak in 1919 and 1920. In those years the cost of living dollar was worth less than 50 cents as compared with the 100 cent dollar of 1914. Following 1920 there was a gradual lowering of the cost of living until December, 1924, then rather a sharp rise to December, 1925.

Table IV of Appendix A shows the trend of the retail cost of food in the United States from 1890 to 1925. This table accepts the 1913 cost of food as the basis and reports the relative cost of equal amounts of food for every other year of this thirty-six year period. For instance, the amount of food which cost $100 in

-49-

1915 could have been bought for $69.60 in 1890 or for $68.70 in 1900, but would have required an expenditure of $203.40 in 1920 or of $157.40 in 1925. All of the figures reported in these two tables are taken from the bulletins of the United States Bureau of Labor Statistics.

Table I shows the computation which was used in fitting together the cost of food index for the period from 1900 to 1914 and the index of the cost of living for New York City from 1914 to December, 1925. It is explained in Chapter II that the Committee, lacking figures on the total cost of living in New York City for the years preceding 1914, used the cost of food in the whole United States in place of the more significant facts which could not be secured.

TABLE I

COMPUTATION OF INDEXES OF COST OF LIVING

Cost of Living in New York City Since 1914 and Country Wide Cost of Food Before 1914 Combined into a Single Index

Based on Data from the United States Bureau of Labor Statistics.

	Cost of Food	Cost of Living	Compared on 1910 Base	Compared on 1900 Base
1900	68.7	—	73.9	100.0
1910	93.0	—	100.0	135.4
1913	100.0	—	107.5	145.5
1914	102.4	100.0	110.1	149.0
Dec. 1924 (New York City) -		176.5	194.3	262.9
Dec. 1925 (New York City) -		183.2	201.7	272.9

In New York City, December, 1925, Dollar was worth 49.57¢ on 1910 Base

In New York City, December, 1925, Dollar was worth 36.61¢ on 1900 Base

When these two indexes are put together it is shown that the purchasing power of the dollar was less than half as great in December, 1925, as in 1910. The actual index was 201.7. If 1900 is used as a basis, this table shows that it required $272.90 to buy as much in December, 1925, as could have been bought for $100 in 1900. In other words, the 1925 dollar was worth less than 37 cents in terms of the 1900 dollar.

The procedure used in determining the average salaries paid to the several groups of teachers in 1900 and in 1910 and in 1925-26 has been explained in Chapter II, page 25 . Table V of the Appendix reports the average salaries paid to men teachers of the different groups in 1910 and at present. In the last column of this table the present salaries are translated into an index number. This index number is the percentage relationship between the purchasing power of present salaries and of the salaries of 1910. Table VI of the Appendix presents corresponding facts for women teachers and Table VII the facts for entire groups of teachers, men and women together. These three tables present facts of very great interest and significance.

It will be noted that not a single group of men teachers or administrators were receiving a salary whose purchasing power was equivalent to the salaries paid in 1910. In Chapter V, page 177, it is reported that the salary schedule for clerical and laboratory assistants is sufficiently high that it has attracted to these positions young men whose educational qualifications are higher than the positions really require. Table V shows that the men in these positions are now receiving an average salary whose purchasing power is almost as great as the salaries of 1910. No other group of men is being paid more than 81 per cent as much as it was receiving in 1910 if present salaries be interpreted in terms of their purchasing power. The men teachers in senior high schools are being paid 78 per cent as much as in 1910. The men who are elementary principals are receiving 69 per cent and those who are high school principals only 64 per cent as much as these groups received in 1910.

An important fact should be kept in mind when considering the relationship between the present salaries of women and the salaries paid in 1910. Equal pay for men and women had not yet been adopted in 1910. Salaries of women at that time were very much lower than the salaries paid to men in corresponding positions. For that reason the index of the purchasing power of the salaries of women is notably higher than the corresponding indexes for the salaries of men.

The largest group of women teachers is to be found teaching in the elementary school grades from kindergarten to 6B. In 1910 there were 11,000 of these women teachers with an average salary of $913. In 1925-26 the number of women elementary teachers had increased beyond 14,000 and the average salary was $2,451. This present salary would buy only as much as $1,215 would buy in 1910. In other words, the effective increase in the salary of women elementary teachers was from $913 to $1,215, an increase in purchasing power of almost exactly one-third.

Two other large groups of women teachers, those in grades 7 to 9 and those in junior high school, are receiving average salaries which are 21 and 30 per cent higher, respectively, than in 1910.

The fourth large group of women teachers - those in senior high school - were receiving an average salary of $1,660 in 1910 and of $3,226 in 1925-26. The purchasing power of this $3,226 salary was equivalent to $1,599 in 1910. In other words, present salaries of women teachers in senior high school are four per cent lower than were the salaries paid to these teachers in 1910, notwithstanding the fact that the principle of equal pay for men and women has gone into effect since 1910. This fact is interesting and conclusive evidence that salary legislation since 1910 has been much more favorable to elementary teachers than to high school teachers.

In 1910 the maximum salary for women principals of elementary schools was only $2,500 while the maximum for men principals was $3,500. Since that time the salary of these women principals has been made the same as that of men, yet the purchasing power of their present salaries is only 92 per cent as great as that of the salaries of 1910.

The only women to whom the adoption of equal pay has not given salaries as great in purchasing power as were the salaries of

1910 are senior high school teachers, principals of elementary school and teacher-clerks in elementary schools.

Table VII, Appendix A shows how the present salaries of entire teaching groups compare with the purchasing power of 1910 salaries. In this table men and women teachers are treated as a single group. It shows that senior high school teachers and both high school and elementary principals are receiving salaries which are in effect much lower than in 1910.

Throughout the discussion of this section it should be remembered that the 1910 salaries, although higher than most of the salaries paid at present, were undoubtedly lower than they ought to have been. Evidence of this is found in the fact that salaries in 1910 were exactly the same as those in 1900, yet the cost of food, and probably the whole cost of living, had increased by one-third during this ten-year period. Additional evidence of the truth of this statement is to be found in the fact that there was much agitation for increased salaries in 1910.

It has been stated in Chapter II, page 28 that the Committee attaches little importance to the index of purchasing power based on the dollar of 1900. Table VIII, Appendix A reports these indexes. The reader may attach to them whatever of importance he may feel is justified. It will be noted in this table that the teachers of atypical children are the only group whose salaries retain the purchasing power of 1900. In no case are men of any one of these groups receiving a present purchasing

-55-

power greater than 60 per cent of that of 1900 with the exception of the clerical and laboratory assistants. The women elementary teachers are now receiving an average salary whose purchasing power is 98 per cent as great as that of the average salary of 1900. Again it will be remembered that there was a wide differential between the salaries of men and women in 1900, and that a comparison of the average salaries then and now is quite misleading.

B. INCREASES IN TEACHERS' SALARIES COMPARED WITH THOSE IN WAGES AND OTHER SALARIES.

One of the minor studies carried on by the Citizens' Committee on Teachers' Salaries was a comparison of the increases in the salaries of teachers in New York City with the corresponding increases in wages and salaries paid in the trades and in other professions. The Research Department of the Federal Reserve Bank of New York has published an index of wages and salaries. A more recent index is reported by Carl Snyder in the December, 1926, issue of the "Journal of the American Statistical Association" * This newer index includes the wages and salaries of many workers not included in the first index. The two indexes are in quite close agreement however - an excellent indication of the validity of each. Chart 4 shows that these indexes from 1919 to the present time have not been more than 6 or 7 points apart - a maximum of three per cent of disagreement.

---
*Journal of American Statistical Association, Vol. XXI, New Series 156, pages 466-470.

CHART 4
TWO COMPOSITE INDEXES OF WAGES IN THE UNITED STATES

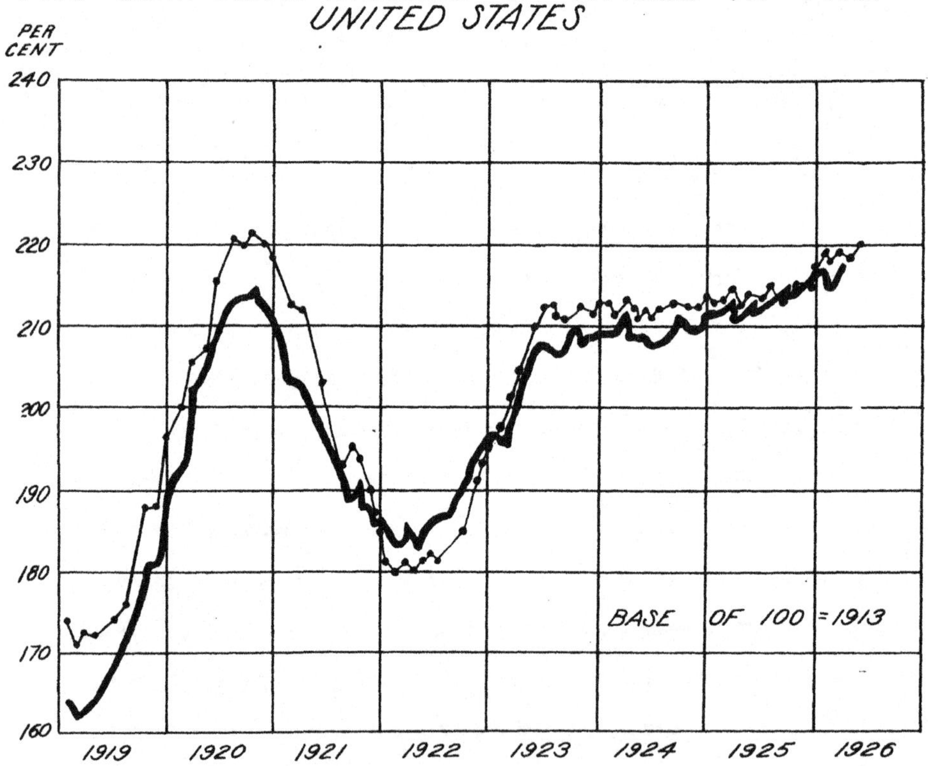

BASE OF 100 = 1913

LEGEND — OLD INDEX OF WAGES
— NEW INDEX OF WAGES

This chart shows that for the last three years wages and salaries on the average have ranged from 2.1 to 2.2 times as high as they were in 1913. This is another way of saying that the average worker is now receiving about $215 for every $100 which he was paid in 1913.

In the preceding section of this chapter it has been shown that the cost of living in New York City is now only 83 per cent higher than it was in 1914. Table IV in the Appendix shows that the cost of food in the country as a whole increased 2.4 per cent from 1913 to 1914. It is reasonable to suppose that the cost of living in New York City increased by about the same amount during that year. If this be true, the cost of living in New York City increased only about 88 per cent from 1913 to December, 1925. In other words, $188 would have gone as far toward meeting the cost of living at the beginning of 1926 as $100 would have gone in 1913. It has just been stated that the average worker was receiving approximately $215 at this time for every $100 received in 1913. In other words, the purchasing power of wages in general was a good deal higher than it was in 1913.

The preceding section of this chapter has shown that the salaries of New York City teachers do not now have as great purchasing power as in 1910. Since the average salary of the New York City teachers was considerably increased upon the adoption of equal pay in 1912 it is evident that the purchasing power of the present salaries is even further below that of 1913 salaries than of 1910 salaries.

In another chart in this same report in the Journal of the American Statistical Association the line of increases in the salaries of school teachers of the United States is reported. This chart is here reproduced as Chart 5. This indicates that school teachers in the United States as a whole are now receiving more than $240 for every $100 which they received in 1913. This is even more important evidence that salaries of New York City teachers have not been increased as rapidly as they should have been. It would be easy to argue that the service rendered by teachers and by other workers was of so different a nature that it was unfair to compare teachers' salaries with these other wages, but it would seem reasonable for New York City teachers to ask that their salaries be increased as rapidly as the salaries of the other teachers of the United States have been increased.

CHART 5
INDEX OF TEACHERS SALARIES IN THE UNITED STATES COMPARED WITH COMPOSITE INDEX OF WAGES IN THE UNITED STATES

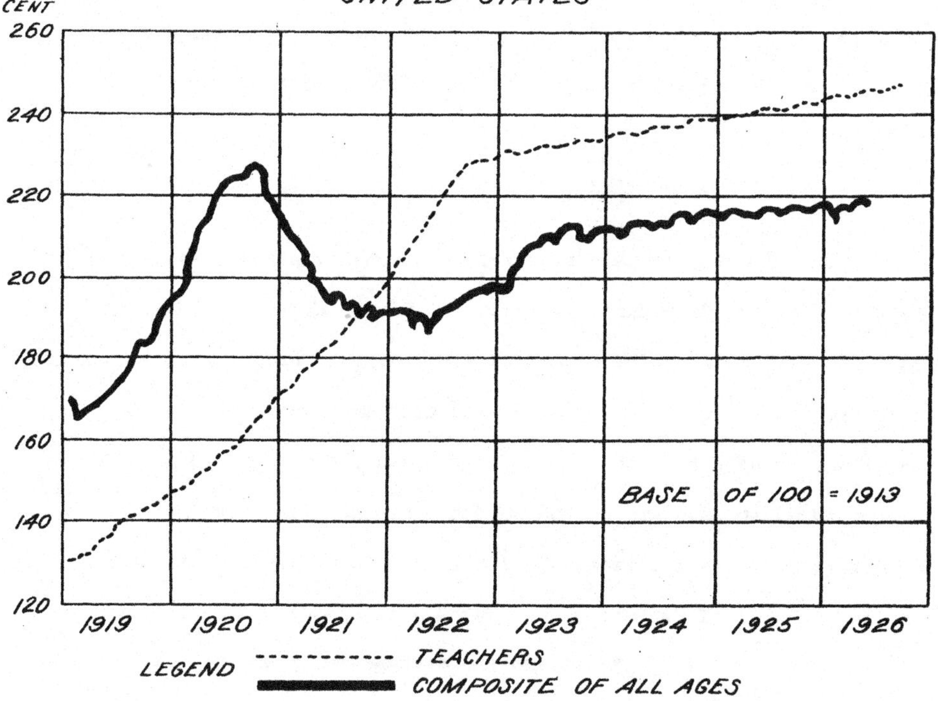

BASE OF 100 = 1913

LEGEND ---------- TEACHERS
        ——— COMPOSITE OF ALL AGES

This second study convinced the Committee that teachers' salaries in New York City have not been increased as rapidly as the teachers had a right to expect, since these increases have kept pace neither with the increases in wages and salaries of other workers nor with the salaries paid to the other teachers of the United States.

It is true that a study of the salaries paid to other municipal and state employees in New York City indicates that the teachers have received greater increases since 1910 than have many of these other groups. The Committee takes the position that the under-payment of other groups of employees does not justify the continued under-payment of school teachers.

C. SALARIES IN OTHER LARGE AMERICAN CITIES.

The Director of this study made personal visits to Washington, Philadelphia, Boston, Cleveland, Detroit, St. Louis, Chicago and Kansas City for the purpose of making a careful study of the teacher salary situation in each of these cities. Particular attention was given to the amounts of salary paid to each teaching group, to the percentage of men teachers employed in each group, and to the bases used in determining salaries in each of these cities. So far as the data were available he studied the salaries of men and women teachers separately. In Washington and Boston it was impossible to secure the average salaries which were paid but even in these cities the minimum and maximum salaries of each schedule were obtained. The salary records in Cleveland were such that the average salaries of men and women separately could not be secured. In St. Louis the average salaries of men and women teachers in the elementary school could not be secured, but the salaries for all other groups of men and women were obtained.

Table IX in Appendix A presents a summary of the average salaries paid to each teaching group in Philadelphia, Cleveland, Detroit, St. Louis, Chicago, Kansas City and New York. In the last column of the table is given the total for each group in the six other cities.

A study of the proportion of men teachers who are employed in these cities is of interest. In the senior high schools of New York City 43 per cent of all the teachers are men. This figure is the same as the average for all six cities. In like manner three per cent of the elementary teachers of New York City are men and the percentage of men elementary teachers in the six cities is exactly the same. In only one teaching position in New York City is there a smaller proportion of men than in these other cities and that is in the junior high school and in grades 7 to 9 - those who are teaching on the so-called "promotion" license. The average for the six cities is 18 per cent of men teachers and in New York City it is only 12 per cent of men. With this exception New York is attracting as large a percentage of men teachers into its school system as are these other cities even if the percentage of men teachers is now a good deal less than it was a few years ago in this city.

As one studies Table IX it will be noted that the average

salaries of practically all teaching groups in other cities are lower than for the corresponding groups in New York City. Notable exception will be found in the case of women high school teachers, women elementary principals, men and women junior high school principals, and associate superintendents of schools in Chicago. Detroit pays the men teachers of atypical children higher salaries than they receive in New York City and Chicago pays both men and women teachers of this group higher salaries than does New York.

It is most unfortunate that there are available no figures concerning the relative cost of living in American cities. Because of this lack the Citizens' Committee was unable to draw any conclusion concerning the relative adequacy of salaries in New York and in other cities. The only evidence which it found, reported in Section B of this chapter, is that the increases in salaries in New York City have not kept pace with the increases of teachers' salaries in the country as a whole.

The principal use which the Committee made of the data concerning salaries in other cities was that of studying the relationship between the salaries of two given groups of teachers in these Cities and in New York. It will be noted, for instance, that the average salary of elementary principals is almost exactly twice that of the average salary of women elementary teachers in nearly all of these cities. This was accepted as an important relationship and was used by the Citizens' Committee as a guide in recommending a schedule for the elementary principals of New York City.

In like manner the inter-relations of the salaries of the higher administrative officers were studied carefully by the Committee in their consideration of the salaries to be recommended for corresponding educational positions in New York City.

Another important relationship which was used in checking the validity of the Committee's recommendations was that of the average senior high school salary to the average elementary school salary in these cities. In half of the cities studied the senior high school salaries were more than 50 per cent higher than elementary salaries and about in half of them less than 50 per cent higher. This fact was accepted as evidence that the proposed schedule for high school teachers in New York City was not disproportionately higher than that proposed for elementary teachers.

Boston is the only city visited which pays men more than women in the same teaching position.

D. THE PROFESSIONAL AND ECONOMIC STATUS OF NEW YOUR CITY TEACHERS.

It has been stated in Chapter II that the Citizens' Committee found it necessary to ask the cooperation of individual teachers in order to secure certain significant facts of direct bearing upon salary problems. A total of 11,081 of these reports were carefully filled out by individual teachers and returned to the Committee. As has been explained, the facts given in each report were expressed in code and two duplicate

Hollerith cards were punched to represent these facts. The Committee has these two sets of 11,000 cards on file and would be able at a few hours' notice to secure any combination of facts which anyone might want to know concerning the teachers of New York City. If it were desired to find out, for instance, the different amounts spent monthly for food by married men who teach history in the senior high schools and who have three children and live in furnished apartments with heat and janitor service supplied and pay an annual rental between $1,000 and $1,300, it would require only two or three hours to secure this information. The Committee actually has tabulated the different amounts spent for food and for rent and the earnings from sources other than the Board of Education during the regular year and during the summer vacation for the married men teachers of each teaching group who have no children, one child, two children, three children, and so on up to a maximum of nine children.

It is not to be implied that all of the facts reported in this section of the report have a direct bearing upon the problem of determining fair and equitable salaries. The mass of data secured by the Committee included many facts of general economic interest and significance which have never before been available for a large group of teachers. Some of these facts will be reported in this section solely because they are of interest and importance even though they have had no bearing upon the Committee's recommendations concerning salaries.

Amount of Professional Preparation

One of the Committee's main reasons for asking the individual teachers to cooperate in this study was the necessity of securing the data concerning their professional training. Since the reports filed in the offices of the Board of Education are of the date when each teacher last appeared for examination, these facts could not be used by the Committee in their study of the present status of New York City teachers.

In the reproduction of the report blank which appears on page 38 will be found the form which each teacher filled out in reporting her professional preparation. This form made it possible for the Committee to determine how many years each teacher had spent in high school, how many years in normal schools or other teacher training institutions, how many years in under-graduate work and how many years in post-graduate work in colleges and universities. A summary of these facts for the men and women of each of 22 teaching groups will be found in Table X of Appendix A. A careful study of this table will be most helpful to any one who is interested in the professional status of New York City teachers.

The statistical average used in this table is the median - the middle case when a given group is arranged in order of the amount of training which they have received. Another way of explaining this average is to say that half of the group has received more and half of the group less than the number of years of training reported in this table. The second column of the table which reports the average number of years of training beyond high school graduation is undoubtedly the most important single column of the table. Whenever the average reported is 0.0 years, it is an indication that fewer than 50 per cent of that particular group of teachers has had any professional training of the type specified at the head of that column.

It will be noted that most of the women who are teaching in elementary schools have had the greater part of their training in normal schools and other teacher training institutions, while the small percentage of this group who are men are largely college trained. This fact holds true both of the teachers and the principals of the elementary schools.

Another interesting comparison which may be made from this table is to be found in the professional preparation of the regular senior high school teachers, or "assistants", as they are called in New York City. The facts concerning these teachers were tabulated separately for those who teach the traditional high school subjects such as language, science, history, and mathematics and for those who teach what may be called the more "modern" subjects - shop work, music, physical education, commercial subjects and the like.

The teachers of these older high school subjects are very definitely college trained. The women have an average of four years of under-graduate work in colleges and universities and almost a year of post-graduate work in colleges and universities. The men teachers of this same group have also had four years of under-graduate study and an average of 1.3 years of post-graduate work. Only a small percentage of either the men or women have had any training in normal schools. Seventy-nine per cent of the women and 90 per cent of the men have had more than four years of training beyond high school graduation.

The assistants who teach the modern subjects are very differently trained. Many of the women assistants have had normal school training of two or more years and half of them have also had as much as two and a half years of under-graduate study in colleges and universities. Only 57 per cent of these women teachers have had more than four years of training beyond high school. The men of this group have had even less of academic training; only 49 per cent of them have had more than four years of training beyond high school graduation. The average for the group is therefore a little less than four years. Only a small percentage of either the men or the women have had any post-graduate work in colleges and universities.

It is an interesting fact that half of the women who are teaching in the elementary schools below the seventh grade have had no more than two and a half years of training beyond high school graduation although the minimum requirement for this group is now three years beyond high school. Of course it is easy to explain this situation - the requirement of three years of training beyond high school has been in effect a comparatively short time. This fact does indicate, however, that only a small proportion of these teachers

have secured professional training beyond the minimum requirement for
their license when they entered the public schools. As a matter of
fact, 39 per cent of all the women elementary teachers now in service
do not report any professional training beyond the two-year minimum
which has been in effect for many years. Only 19 per cent of these
teachers have had more than four years of study since graduating from
high school. It was facts such as these which led the Committee to
recommend the immediate adoption of a super-maximum salary for all
teachers who have secured as much as one year of training beyond
the minimum requirement for their license.

   Only one of the 194 elementary principals who reported to
the Committee had less than two years of professional training. Seventy
nine per cent of the women and 86 per cent of the men of this group
reported more than four years training beyond high school graduation.
The women principals have received the majority of their training in
teacher training institutions and the men principals are very largely
college trained. Half of the men have had as much as one and a half
years of post-graduate work in colleges and universities. The women
principals average a half year less of professional preparation than
do the men but both groups are very well trained so far as can be
judged from the number of years they have spent in professional study.

   On page 170 of this report the Citizens' Committee suggests
that the position of assistant to elementary principals should be considered by the Board of Education as the best possible training for

those to be chosen to fill vacancies in elementary principalships.
A study of the training of the present assistants to elementary
principals is convincing evidence of the soundness of this suggestion.
Table   shows that both the men and the women are very largely normal
school trained and that 50 per cent of the men have had the equivalent
of college graduation in addition to two years in normal schools. These
facts indicate that a very large percentage of this group of assistants has had the combination of professional training which is most
commonly accepted as ideal for a principal of elementary school. Not
only do these persons have the cultural background which is expected
to be secured through years of college and university training but they
also have had an average of two years of normal school training in
how to teach and supervise and build courses of study in the field of
elementary education. It will be noted that the men who are now elementary principals, drawn largely as they were from high school teaching, do not have a definite professional preparation in the field in
which they serve except as they have secured it through post-graduate
work at colleges and universities. Over and above these facts concerning professional training it must be accepted that the professional experience of these elementary assistants is much more directly
related to the elementary principalship than is high school teaching.

At the end of Table X on page 235, Appendix A, is presented
a summary of the average training of all men and women who replied to
the Committee's inquiry. This summary shows that half of the women

teachers did not have more than three years of training beyond high school while half of the men have 4.9 years of training. It should be remembered that these facts do not imply that men teachers are better trained than women teachers in corresponding professional positions. On the contrary, it is almost equivalent to a statement that high school teachers have more years of training than elementary teachers - a fact which is known and accepted by every one. This results because a large proportion of the total number of women are elementary teachers while a great majority of the men who reported are high school teachers.

For this summary of the table the tabulation cards have been sorted according to the economic status of the men and women teachers. It will be noted that the unmarried women living away from home have more years of training, and a larger percentage who are college graduates, than have either of the other two groups of women. This probably results from the fact that nearly 40 per cent of the women teachers in high school live away from home while only 20 per cent of the women elementary teachers are so situated.

It is entirely impossible to discuss in detail the many other interesting and important facts which are available in this study of the professional training of those in the public schools of New York City. Careful study of Table X will reveal many others which cannot even be mentioned in this section.

Amount of Teaching Experience

Another phase of the Committee's study which was based on the reports of individual teachers was of great importance in helping the Committee to determine the distinguishing characteristics of the different teaching groups. This was the report of each teacher concerning the number of years of her teaching service.

The teachers reported the total number of years taught in the public schools and the number of years taught outside the public schools of New York City. The interpretation of these facts resulted in two important discoveries. One was the perfectly obvious conclusion concerning the amount of teaching experience, with its implications as to the ages of the teachers in different groups, and the other was authoritative information concerning the percentage of teachers who had never taught outside the New York City public schools. This second fact was of great significance in describing the different teaching groups.

Table XI in Appendix A, page 236, reports these facts for all of the regular day school teachers of the city. In each case the total teaching group is divided into the six economic groups mentioned above, three of women and three of men. The average reported in this table is again the middle case - half of each group had more and half had less teaching experience than the figure reported as the average. This table also reports the range of the middle 50 per cent of each group as to their teaching experience. In the top line of the table, it is shown, for instance, that the 4,569 women of the elementary school who reported to the Committee showed a range from 4.7 to 9.0 years in the middle 50 per cent of the group. In other words, one-fourth of this group of women have taught less than 4.7 years and another fourth have taught more than 19 years. The middle amount of teaching service for this group was 9.7 years.

The last column of this same table reports some startling facts. Eighty-seven per cent of the women and 89 per cent of the men elementary school teachers have never taught a single day outside of the public schools of New York City. That this situation is a very serious one is indicated by the fact that a very large proportion of the younger women in this group are classified in the economic group of those who are unmarried and living at home and that 95 per cent of this group have had their total teaching experience in the public schools of New York City, indicating that this percentage is undoubtedly increasing. This provincialism of the New York City teachers is not quite so marked in the case of teachers of junior high school and grades 7 to 9. In this group, however, 85 per cent of the women and 78 per cent of the men teachers have had their entire teaching experience within the public schools of New York City. In the senior high schools there has been decidedly less of this inbreeding, yet fifty-seven per cent of the women high school teachers and 66 per cent of the men have had no teaching experience outside of the city public schools.

In discussing the Committee's procedure in determining salary schedules, in Chapter V of this report, it is pointed out that in the case of elementary teachers, unmarried women living away from home and in the case of senior high school teachers married men were chosen as the basic groups. The facts concerning the amount of teaching experience presented in Table indicates that these groups whose living costs were highest are likewise the groups who have the longest periods of service in the New York City schools. The women elementary teachers who are unmarried and living away from home have an average of 19 years of teaching experience. One-fourth of them have been teaching more than 27 years. The married women of this group have an average of 13 years of teaching experience while the unmarried women living at home have an average of less than seven years experience. In the case of the men teachers in senior high school the married men have been longest in service, one-fourth of them having taught more than 24 years and one-half of them more than 15 years.

In all groups the unmarried teachers living at home, whether men or women, are the youngest in point of service. The youngest of all are the unmarried men who are teaching in elementary school. Half of them have less than three years of teaching experience. It will be remembered that many of these young men are college graduates, as reported in the preceding section of this chapter. These two facts, taken together, indicate quite clearly that these young men are not permanent members of the elementary teaching group. Very evidently they are using teaching in the elementary schools as a stepping stone to some other profession or business.

The first column of Table XI presents some interesting facts concerning the economic status of each of these groups of teachers. More than half of the women elementary teachers are unmarried and living at home. Less than one-fifth of them are married women. About 25 per cent of these women elementary teachers who made reports to the Committee are unmarried women who are living away from home. Included in this group are many of the older teachers, as was mentioned above, and approximately one-third of them have had some teaching experience outside of the public schools of New York City. The oldest group, in point of service, of the regular teachers of New York City is found to be the women teachers in junior high school and in grades 7 to 9 who are unmarried and living away from home. Half of this group has had more than 24 years and a fourth of them more than 30 years. The youngest group is made up of the men elementary teachers who are unmarried and living at home.

A Study of Teachers' Dependents

One of the questions of the voluntary report made by individual teachers was, "How many persons, not including yourself, are chiefly dependent on your income?" Married teachers who were living with wife or husband were also asked: "How many children have you?" The tabulation of the answers to these two questions yielded most interesting and significant facts concerning the economic status of the New York City teachers. Seventy per cent of the women and 91 per cent of the men teachers reported one or more persons beside themselves who were chiefly dependent upon their incomes. Table XIII of Appendix A, page 239, summarizes these facts for all of the men and women who are teachers in the regular day schools of the city. Chart 6 expresses these same facts in graphic form.

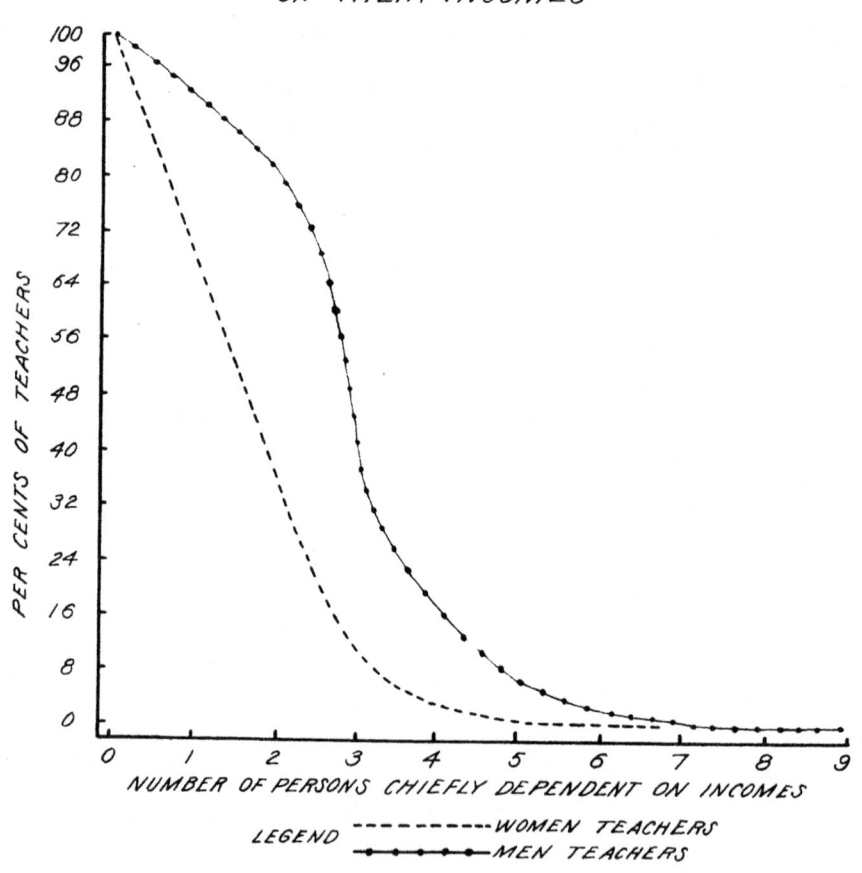

CHART 6
PER CENTS OF MEN AND WOMEN TEACHERS HAVING INDICATED NUMBER OF PERSONS CHIEFLY DEPENDENT ON THEIR INCOMES

In general, it may be stated that men teachers have one or two more persons dependent upon their income than have women teachers. This table shows for instance that 70 per cent of all the women have one or more persons dependent upon them while 70 per cent of the men have two or more dependents. Thirty-six per cent of the women have two or more dependents and forty per cent of the men have three or more dependents. Eleven per cent of the women have three or more dependents while 18 per cent of the men have four or more dependents, and six per cent of the men have five or more dependents.

The Committee tabulated the data concerning dependents in such a way that it might study the variation in number of dependents with the age of the teachers upon whom they were dependent. Since the Committee did not presume to ask teachers to report their age, it was necessary to use the number of years of teaching experience as an index of age. Each group of teachers was divided into three sub-groups according to the number of years they had taught - those who have taught less than ten years, those who have taught from 10 to 25 years, and those who have taught more than 25 years.

In the case of women teachers it was found that the number of persons who were dependent neither increased nor decreased appreciably with increasing years of service. Chart 7 shows this fact in graphic form. It will be seen that the three lines which represent these groups of teachers of different ages very nearly coincide throughout. Table XIII of the Appendix, upon which this chart is based, shows that 35 per cent of the youngest group, 29 per cent of the oldest group and only 25 per cent of those who have taught from 10 to 25 years have no dependents at all. Three per cent of each of the three groups has three or more dependents.

Quite a different situation is found in the case of men teachers. The younger men - those who have taught less than 10 years - do not have so many dependents as have the two older groups of men. There is a slight falling off in the number of dependents in the case of men who have been teaching more than 25 years but the decrease is a very small one. Chart 8 shows graphically these facts for men teachers just as Chart 7 pictures the variation in the number of dependents of women teachers. It will be noted that the inside line of this chart is that which represents the facts concerning the younger men.

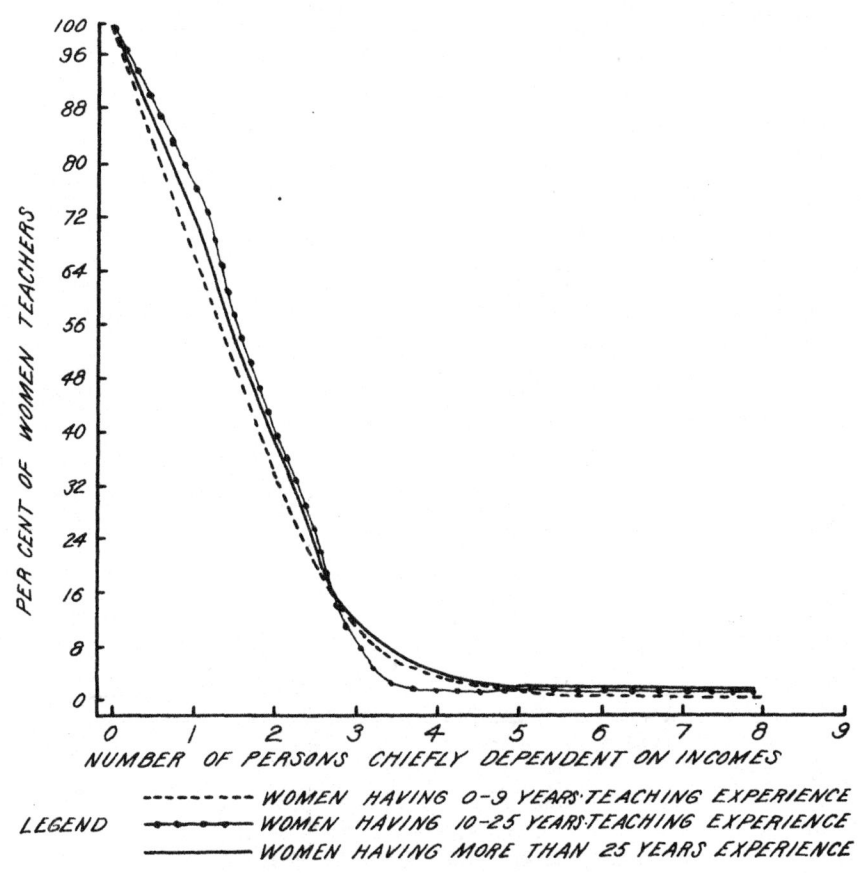

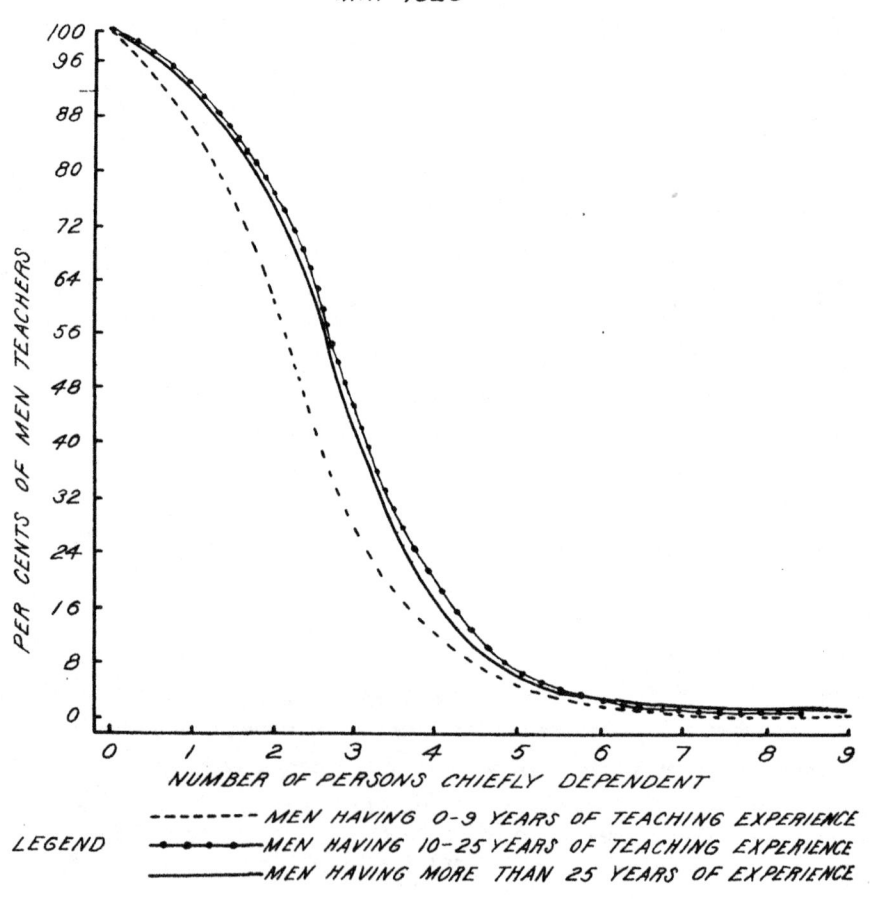

The next table in Appendix A, Table XII on page 238, shows the facts concerning the dependents of the several economic groups of teachers. Each of these groups is again sub-divided according to number of years of teaching service. It is an interesting fact that the married women report fewer dependents than do either the unmarried women who are living at home or those who are living away from home. Thirty-four per cent of the married women do not report any dependents. Twenty-nine per cent of the unmarried women living at home and 27 per cent of the women living away from home do not report any dependents. Exactly 36 per cent of each of these three groups of women report two or more dependents. A slightly larger percentage of the married women report three and four and five dependents.

As would be expected, the facts are very different with respect to men teachers. Ninety-seven per cent of the married men report one or more dependents but 25 per cent of the unmarried men have no dependents at all. The unmarried men who are living at home have more dependents than unmarried women living at home but there is practically no difference in the number of dependents of the men and women who are living away from home.

A study of the number of dependents of the women teachers in each type of regular day school is reported in Table XII of Appendix A, page 238. This table shows that the women elementary teachers have fewer dependents than other women teachers, but the difference is not great. The married women who teach in senior high school have a greater number of dependents than any other economic group of women teachers. Twenty-nine per cent of these married women have three or more dependents. Not more than 11 per cent of any other large group of women teachers have so heavy an economic burden.

This table makes possible a very interesting comparison which has a direct bearing upon the Committee's salary recommendations. In computing the schedule of salaries for elementary teachers the Committee accepted unmarried women who were living away from home as the basic group. In the determination of the salary schedule for senior high school teachers, married men who have a wife and one child were chosen as the basic group. Table XII shows that 73 per cent of the women elementary teachers living away from home have one or more dependents, 38 per cent have two or more and 10 per cent have three or more dependents. In comparison with these figures, 50 per cent of the married men who teach in senior high school have three or more dependents - that is they have one or more dependents beyond the equivalent of a wife and child. Twenty-three per cent of these men have four or more dependents and nine per cent have five or more dependents. In other words, nine per cent of this basic group of married men teachers have the equivalent of a wife and child and three or more additional dependents, while in the basic group used in figuring the elementary teachers' schedule, 10 per cent have a total of three or more dependents beside themselves. The Citizens' Committee accepts this fact as important evidence that its choice of these two basic groups was entirely fair and impartial.

Number of Children of Married Teachers

A study of the replies to the question, "How many children have you?" shows that 74 per cent of the married men and 43 per cent of the married women teachers have one or more children. Seventy-seven per cent of the married men who teach in senior high school have one or more children, 46 per cent have two or more and seven per cent of these high school men have four or more children. One teacher reported a total of nine children. Fifty per cent of the married men teaching in elementary school have no children. Seventy-eight per cent of the married men who teach in junior high school and in grades 7 to 9 have one or more children. Forty-seven per cent have two or more and nine per cent have four or more children. Twenty-three per cent of all of the married men who are teaching in the regular day schools have one or more dependents in addition to their wives and children. The number of children reported by married men of each teaching group is shown in Table XXII Appendix A, page 251.

The Earnings of New York City Teachers

An important phase of the Committee's study of the reports made by individual teachers was concerned with the earnings of each group from sources other than the Board of Education. These earnings were reported under two headings: (1) earnings from sources other than Board of Education during the regular school year, and (2) earnings from outside sources during the summer vacation. The Committee attaches especial importance to the first of these items on the theory that those who depend upon additional sources of income during the regular school year are in a very real sense part-time teachers. It should be remembered that the facts given in this section do not include the earnings of regular day school teachers who also teach in evening schools. The income from evening school teaching is a part of the money paid to the teacher by the Board of Education.

In this study, as in all of the studies of teachers relating to their economic status, the married men teachers were classified into ten groups according to whether they had no children, one child, and so on up to the maximum of nine children.

The Committee finds that 28 per cent of all of the men who are teaching in the regular day schools are earning money from sources other than the Board of Education during the regular school year. Only 11 per cent of these men reported earnings from such sources during the summer vacation.

Further analysis of these figures reveals some very interesting facts. Twenty per cent of the men elementary teachers have sources of income during the regular school year in addition to their teacher's salaries. Those who are thus employed have an average income from outside sources of $415 a year. Nine per cent of these men earn an average of $197 during the summer vacation. In the case of the men who teach in grades 7 to 9 and in the junior high schools, 31 per cent of the whole group earn an average of $680 a year in addition to their regular salaries during the school year and eleven per cent of these men find employment during the summer which yields them an average of $622. The average earnings of this group of men from all sources, their regular salaries included, amounts to $3,270 per year.

Twenty-nine per cent of the men teachers in senior high school have earnings from outside sources during the regular year. These earnings average $731 a year for those who have such outside employment. Twelve per cent of these senior high school men earn an average of $506 in the summer. The average income of these men from all sources is $3,722.

The percentage of married men who have outside employment during the regular year is slightly higher than the corresponding percentage for unmarried men. In the case of these married men there are 21 per cent of elementary school teachers, 32 per cent of the junior high school and 7th to 9th grade teachers, and 33 per cent of the senior high school teachers who have other income during the regular school year.

Table XVI in Appendix A, p.244, reports the earnings of these married men who have different numbers of children. It is there shown that 50 per cent of the married men in junior high school who have three children are on part time and earn an average of $613 during the regular school year in addition to their salary. Thirty-five per cent of these men who have two children and 34 per cent of those who have one child earn an average of $653 and $510 respectively during the regular year.

In the senior high school the largest percentage of the married men with children who have outside employment during the regular school year is the group having two children. Thirty-nine per cent of these men are employed and their average earnings are $692 a year. Thirty-seven per cent of those who have three children, 34 per cent of those with four children, and 29 per cent of those having one child are also on part time in the sense in which that term is employed in this discussion. Those with four children have an average income from outside sources of $886 a year. Those with three children average $1,316. The earnings of the other married men who teach in senior high school and have found outside employment range from $600 to $850 per year.

A careful study of Table XV will yield many more interesting and significant facts concerning the economic status of the men teachers of New York City. A much smaller percentage of the women teachers have earnings from outside sources either during the school year or during the summer vacation. Only six per cent of the total group of regular teachers have earnings from outside sources during the regular year and two per cent during the summer vacation, as compared with 28 per cent and 11 per cent, respectively, of the men teachers.

In general, the income of the women teachers from such sources is less than that of the men teachers. Five per cent of the women elementary teachers earn an average of $130 during the regular year. The other 95 per cent report no income except from the Board of Education. The same percentage of the women teachers in junior high school and in grades 7 to 9 report additional income but the average for the group is $724 a year, a greater amount per person employed than was reported for the men of the same teaching group, but there was six times as large a percentage of men who had found outside employment.

The largest percentage of women teachers who have an income from outside sources during the regular school year is in senior high school. Thirteen per cent of these women earn an average of $321 per year.

The full detail of the earnings of women teachers from all sources is reported in Table XV of Appendix A, page 242. Approximately one-fourth of elementary school teachers earn an average of $1,100 in addition to their salaries during the regular school year, and approximately 15 per cent of them earn an average of $750 during the summer.

Only seven per cent of the women elementary principals have any earnings during the regular year beyond their regular salaries from the Board of Education. Those who are employed average about $1,100, as do the men principals of elementary schools.

Of the 275 teacher clerks who reported to the Committee, only 18 have outside employment during the regular year. These 18 persons, approximately seven per cent of the total, average a little less than $380 a year in addition to their regular salaries.

Of the 176 men and 54 women attendance officers who cooperated with the Committee, eight men and one woman average between $700 and $800 during the school year in addition to their Board of Education salaries. One man reported summer earnings of $1,000 and another of $150. None of the others of this group reported any income during the summer except from the Board of Education.

Facts such as those reported above were secured for many other groups of administrative and supervisory officials. It is impossible within the space available in this report to present detailed facts concerning them.

Annual Rentals Paid By New York City Teachers

In other sections of this report it is stated that the Committee accepted the annual expenditure for the two items of food and rent as an index of the total cost of living of New York City teachers. In order to secure valid figures concerning the cost of rent it was necessary to make a detailed study of many separate factors. Some teachers lease more rooms than they need for themselves and their families and sub-rent to others the extra rooms. Some of the rentals reported are for furnished apartments and some for unfurnished apartments. In some cases heat and janitor service are supplied, in other cases the teacher herself must stand this expense. Recognizing in advance the complications which would be involved, in the confidential report blank sent out to individual teachers the Committee asked for detailed information concerning these different factors in the annual expense for rent.

These reports were then tabulated in such a way that the effect of these variables could be studied.

It was assumed that the men and women teachers who were living at home with parents or married brothers or sisters would not as a rule be held responsible for the renting and sub-renting of the family home so these economic groups were asked simply to report the amount of the annual rent which they themselves paid. On the other hand, married teachers and those living away from home were asked how many rooms they leased and at what annual rental and how many of these rooms were sub-rented and the amount received from such sub-rental.

A total of 3,158 women and 1,311 men in these two groups of the regular teachers in the day schools reported in full the facts concerning the rentals paid and received. Only 285 of the women teachers and 114 of the men teachers, less than 10 per cent in each case, reported an income from sub-rentals. The other 90 per cent of these teaching groups occupied in full the rooms which they rented.

A separate study was made of the rentals paid by the 10 per cent and by the 90 per cent of these two groups. These facts are reported in Table XVII, Appendix A, page 245. This table shows that approximately six per cent of the married women teaching in elementary schools sub-rented rooms. The average rent paid by this six per cent was $1,047 per year and the average income from sub-rented rooms was $420 a year. The average annual rental paid by the 94 per cent of these married women elementary teachers who do not sub-rent rooms was $910. One-fourth of this group paid an annual rental of less than $750 and one-fourth of more than $1,091.

Between eight and nine per cent of the women elementary teachers living away from home reported income from sub-rented rooms. The average rental which they paid was $947 and they received an average of $356 a year from sub-rentals. The women of this group who did not sub-rent rooms paid an annual rental of $691. The average rental paid by the married men of this group who do not sub-rent rooms was $989 per year. Half of them paid between $800 and $1,200 annually for rent.

Table XVIII in the Appendix summarizes the facts concerning the rentals paid and the sub-rentals received by all of the men and women teachers of the regular day schools. It shows that the 114 men teachers who sub-rent rooms pay out an average of $1,279 a year and receive back an average of $418 a year in sub-rents. The difference between these averages is $861 a year. Twenty-five per cent of this group of men pay less than $1,008 and receive not to exceed $258 a year in sub-rents, leaving a net difference of $750.

In the case of the 285 women teachers who sub-rent rooms, the annual rental paid out is an average of $1,021 and the annual income from sub-rented rooms is $396. The difference in these averages is $625. This seems to be a fair figure to represent the net cost of annual rental for those who undertake the responsibility of sub-renting a part of the space which they lease since the middle 50 per cent of the group pay between $820 and $1,400 a year and receive back between $240 and $615 in sub-rentals.

The Committee's study of the relative amounts of rent paid for different types of housing accomodations was confined to the married men teachers on the ground that this group was sufficiently homogeneous that their housing accomodations would be reasonably comparable. A total of 1,171 married men reported the rentals which they paid for different types of accomodations. A little less than three per cent of these men rented furnished rooms or apartments which were heated and had janitor service. The average annual rental paid for such accomodations was $943. Nearly 40 per cent of the total group rented unfurnished rooms or apartments with heat and janitor service supplied. The annual rental paid was $869 on the average, a different of $76 per year. It is highly probable that the married men with small families, for instance those who are young and newly married, are much more likely to rent furnished rooms and apartments than are those whose families have been longer established. It is not to be implied from the figures given above that it costs only $76 more per year to secure a furnished apartment than to secure an unfurnished apartment of the same size.

The third entry in Table XIX is of particular interest because it undoubtedly represents the annual rentals paid by those who live in houses in the suburbs rather than in city apartments. The description "unfurnished, not heated, no janitor service", applies accurately to this particular group. It seems clear that teachers living in the suburbs are paying about $200 per year more for rent than are those who live in city apartments. The same caution must be used in comparing these figures as in comparing the rental paid for furnished and unfurnished apartments. It is undoubtedly true that teachers with the greater number of children will be more willing to undergo the troubles and loss of time of commuting daily than would those without children or with one or two very young children. Probably the average rental of $1,113 paid by this group secures a greater number of rooms than do the average rentals paid for city apartments

The Committee analyzed the rentals paid by New York City teachers from two other points of view. In the first, reported in Table XX of Appendix A, page 248, all the groups of teachers and administrative and supervisory officials of the school system were thrown into a single group and redistributed into 11 groups according to their annual salaries. The average annual rental paid by each salary group was computed. In this table no distinction is made between men and women teachers but the facts are reported separately for (1) the men and women who are married; (2) all those who are unmarried but living at home; (3) for all those who are living away from home.

It is found that married teachers who receive between $1,500 and $2,000 are paying on the average $800 a year for rent but that those of the same salary group who are living at home

-93-

contribute less than $400 a year toward the family rental. Those of this group who are living away from home report an average rental of $566 per year.

With one or two exceptions it is found that the higher salaried groups pay higher rentals, but that the proportion of the salary which is taken up in rent decreases as the salary increases. For instance, married teachers whose salaries are less than $2,000 spend an average of $800 a year for rent, a full 40 per cent of the total salary. On the other hand, those whose annual earnings exceed $5,000 expend only 25 per cent of their income on this item of the annual budget. The same rule holds in the other economic groups.

The Committee's other analysis of annual rentals divided the total number of teachers according to their teaching positions, and studied the men and women of each of the three economic groups separately. Table XXIII, Appendix A, page 251, reports these facts for the teachers in the regular day schools. The most striking fact brought out by this particular study is the large proportion of teachers who are paying less than $200 a year in annual rental. In the case of all of these teaching groups, half of the economic groups made up of either men or women who are unmarried and living at home contribute less than $200 per year to the family rental. In the case of the elementary teachers these teachers living at home make up so large a proportion of the total teaching group that the average rental paid by the whole group is less than $200.

The valid explanation of this figure must be that the families of these teachers donate annually the equivalent of $500 to $800 toward their living expense.

It is interesting to note that the married men who teach in the elementary school expend an average of only $664 per year for rent while the unmarried women living away from home expend $707. Unmarried men living away from home expend much less - an average of only $475 per year.

This table shows that the married men who teach in junior high school spend an average of a little over $900 per year for rent while those married men who teach in senior high school spend $100 a year more for this item. Other interesting facts will be found in a study of this table in Appendix A.

Expenditures for Food

It will be recalled that the second item which was accepted by the Committee as a part of the index of the total cost of living was the cost of food. Table XXI, Appendix A, page 249, reports a complete analysis of this expense on the part of all of the groups of teachers in the regular day schools. The women teachers of each group are sub-divided into the three economic groups used as a basis of discussion in the other sections of this chapter. The men teachers were divided into the corresponding groups, but the married men were further sub-divided according to the number of children in the family.

Chart 9 expresses in graphic form the greater cost of food in families with the greater number of children. The lowest line of this chart cuts off below it the quarter of the married men with each specified number of children whose expense for food was lowest. The highest line of the chart cuts off in like manner the quarter of each group which spends the greatest amount for food. The middle line divides each of these groups into exact halves. It is an interesting fact that these three lines are almost exactly parallel although they are curved. The chart makes it clear that the proportional increase per child is greater in families having one or two children than in families with three or four children. The fact that all of these lines rise more rapidly when there are more than four children in the family is probably accounted for by the fact that in large families such as these at least some of the children will be old enough that they consume almost as much food as an adult.

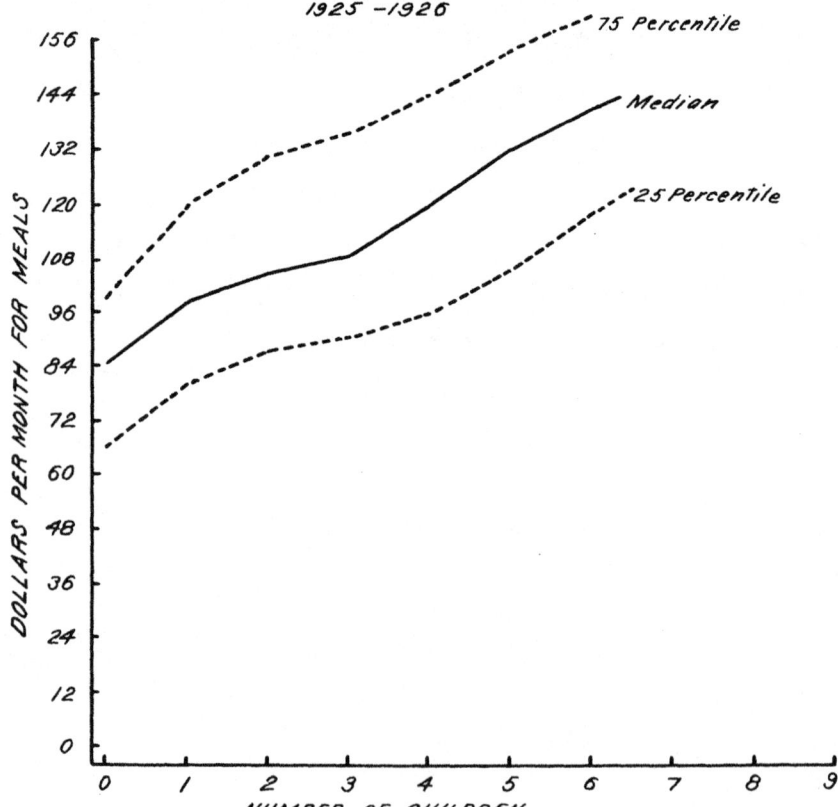

As in the case of rentals paid it will be noted that the higher salaried groups expend more for food. Since the Committee was unable to make a study of the amounts and quality of food consumed, it is not able to state whether the higher salaried groups are extravagant or whether the lower salaried groups are spending less than they should for this important item in the cost of living.

It will be noted in Table XXI, Appendix A, page 249, that the men and women elementary teachers spend almost exactly the same amounts for food. Half of the women expend between $38 and $79 per month and half of the men elementary teachers between $34 and $80. The vaerage expenditure of the women is $52 per month and that of the men $53 per month.

It is significant to note the increased cost of food in the families of married teachers with greater numbers of children. Practically none of the married men teachers in elementary school have more than two children. The average monthly expense for food for those without children is $75, for those with one child, $82 and for those with two children $98 per month.

This same relationship will be noted in the groups of married men teachers in junior and senior high schools. In the junior high school the married men without children report an average of $79 per month. In families with one child the monthly expense is $10 greater and another $10 per month is added for the second child.

In the senior high school the same general relationship holds, except that married men with one child and married men with two children have the same average expenditure for meals - $100 per month. This equality of averages undoubtedly results from the tendency to report as an even $100 amounts anywhere from $95 to $105. A study of the range of the middle 50 per cent of food expenses for these groups shows the usual tendency for increasing cost with an increasing number of children. It will be noted that the increase in monthly expenditure because of one child in the family is usually considerably more than half of the increase on account of two children. This tendency was noted in Chart 9, in the more rapid rise of the three lines at the left side of the chart.

The Committee accepted the complete consistency of these food expense figures as a most important evidence of the accuracy of the reports of the individual teachers. Such complete agreement of these trend lines in all groups of teachers would have been most extraordinary or entirely impossible if the individual teachers had simply made wild guesses concerning their food expenses.

E. ATTRACTIVENESS OF NEW YORK CITY SALARIES TO OUTSIDE TEACHERS

The Citizens' Committee secured two types of evidence as to the attractiveness of public school positions in New York City to teachers from outside the city. One of these was a series of statements from teacher training institutions outside the city concerning the tendency of their graduates to seek positions in New York City. The second type of evidence was the statistical facts concerning the percentage of New York City teachers who have had teaching experience outside of the city.

Replies to the letters of inquiry addressed to heads of teacher training institutions were in general agreement that very small numbers of their graduates were entering the New York City schools. The reason most commonly given, however, gave the Committee no reason for concluding that present salaries were too low to be attractive. Most of these educators agreed that their graduates were staying out of New York City because it seemed to be the administrative policy of the Board of Education to discourage their entrance. Some of the specific points made in these letters referred to the administrative red tape in connection with the teacher examination system, and to the fact that these examinations often were held at such a time in the school year that neither training school students nor teachers in service were able to present themselves for examination.

The second type of evidence secured by the Committee concerning the drawing power of public school positions in New York City has already been presented in some detail in the preceding section on the years of service of the several groups of teachers. It was there stated that only 12 per cent of the women and 11 per cent of the men who teach in the kindergarten and first six grades have ever taught a single day outside of the public schools of the city. In the largest group of young teachers in the elementary schools - unmarried women living at home - only five per cent have had teaching experience elsewhere. Eighty-one per cent of all the women and 72 per cent of all the men teachers in the regular day schools have taught only in the New York City public schools.

   The Committee does not feel justified in asserting that this small percentage of teachers drawn from outside the city is proof that present salaries are too low. This situation could have resulted, as was implied by the letters from heads of teacher training institutions, from the negative policy on the part of the Board of Education with respect to the encouragement of strong candidates from outside the city.

CHAPTER IV

THE BASIC ASSUMPTIONS

The preceding chapters of this report have discussed in some detail the history of teacher salary legislation for New York City, the organization of the Citizens' Committee on Teachers' Salaries, and the Committee's five-fold plan of attack upon the problem. In Chapter III are presented summaries of the facts secured in each of the five studies carried through by the Committee. It was a long step between securing such facts as are reported in the preceding chapter and the determination of actual salary schedules to be recommended to the Board of Education. The whole theory and practice of schedule making had to be studied carefully and the wisest possible choices had to be made in the light of unique local situations. The Committee does not deny that some other body working just as honestly and open-mindedly might have recommended plans of procedure quite different than those which are here recommended. It is the function of this chapter of the report to present and explain the theories and assumptions which were accepted as basic in the Committee's procedure.

A. COMMONLY ACCEPTED BASES FOR SCHEDULES

The Committee's study of the payment of teachers in other cities showed that the salary of an individual teacher may be based upon almost any possible combination of several objective and subjective measures of her professional qualifications and of the importance of her professional position.

Among the objective measures in use are: (1) the number of years she has taught; (2) the number of years of academic or professional preparation she has secured; (3) the grade or type of school in which she teaches; and (4) her sex. Commonly used subjective measures - that is, those which are determined on the basis of the personal opinion of authorized representatives of the Board of Education - are these: (1) her efficiency rating, or teaching-quality rating as determined by one or more of the supervisory or administrative officers of the school system; (2) her ability to pass, or to obtain certain scores, on examinations which may be written or oral, or an actual teaching test, or any combination of these three; and (3) the kind or quality of academic or professional preparation she may have secured, as is required under regulations demanding certain amounts of "approved" training.

Another basis for determining salaries which is sometimes proposed and defended is that of the number of children or the number of dependents which a teacher may have. This idea seems to be borrowed from southwestern Europe where some hundreds of thousands, of miners especially, are paid a family wage.

It is argued by some that the economic law of supply and demand should be the sole consideration in paying salaries to teachers: that boards of education should set up definite minimum qualifications for each type of teaching position, and then should go out into the market and employ at the lowest possible salary those who meet these professional requirements.

Others defend the payment of teachers upon the basis of the importance of the service which they render. Still others would have teachers' salaries take into account the number of hours in the teacher's school day, or the number of weeks in her school year. Probably there is no problem demanding solution by the American public today in which there is a greater confusion of conflicting theories and practices than in this field of determining salary schedules for public school teachers.

The Single Salary Schedule

In recent years a considerable number of Boards of Education have adopted a new plan for determining the salaries which shall be paid to teachers. The schedule of payments based upon this plan is called a single salary schedule. This name is somewhat misleading, but has been generally accepted. In January, 1925, six cities of more than 100,000 population - Denver, Des Moines, Minneapolis, San Antonio, Spokane and Youngstown - were paying teachers on a single schedule. There were more than 100 others in which this plan was in effect.

Denver is a notable example of the successful operation of this newer plan. This plan has been in operation four or five years and all of the teachers of Denver, both elementary and high school, accept the plan most enthusiastically.

The outstanding difference between the single salary schedule and all other schedules in common use is its acceptance of all teaching positions, whether in the kindergarten, the seventh grade, or in the senior high school, as of equal importance and as worthy of equal remuneration. Under this plan differentials in salaries are determined solely on the basis of the professional qualifications of the individual teacher. In general practice only two measures of professional qualifications are taken into consideration: First, the number of years of academic and professional preparation beyond high school graduation; and second, the number of years of teaching experience. It is entirely possible to add to these fundamental measures some others such as the score which a teacher receives when her teaching efficiency or ability are rated by superior officers, or a requirement that her professional preparation be of a certain quality as well as of a certain quantity - that is, that she shall have a certain minimum amount of "approved" professional preparation for the position which she holds.

Probably the soundest principle which may be defended as a basis for determining the amount of a teacher's salary would be her actual teaching efficiency - a measure of how well she actually does the job which she is chosen to do and held responsible for doing. If this indefinite quality or characteristic could be measured objectively, as age or weight or height can be measured, probably most persons would agree that school administrators could throw into the discard all consideration of professional preparation, years of teaching experience and other commonly accepted determiners of teachers' salaries. If such an instrument for measuring teaching ability were available, boards of education could then set up qualifications solely in terms of the individual's score on this measuring device, and then could determine the salaries which they would pay on the basis of the workings of the law of supply and demand with respect to prospective teachers who could measure up to these standard qualifications.

Such an objective measure of teaching ability is entirely lacking. It is entirely possible that it will not be available for many years to come. We do not yet agree as to just what the product of public education is, or ought to be, in any objective sense. We do know that pupils in school acquire certain skills, like ability to read and to spell and to perform certain operations with numbers. We know that there are many bits of information, facts concerning history and geography and literature, a few of which any individual pupil learns to know. In addition to acquiring these skills and facts there are many most important ideas and ideals and character traits which we have a pious hope will in some way grow out of each child's schooling. Important as they are in society, these ideals and traits are vague and not yet subject to objective measure, yet it is the instilling of these vague and unmeasurable qualities which most people would defend as the most valuable service of the teacher.

If, then, we are as yet entirely unable to measure the product of education, it becomes almost absurd to assume that we can now measure the teacher's efficiency in turning out that product. Even if we could measure the product, other difficult problems would face us in measuring teaching efficiency, for the home and the church and all the rest of society are playing their parts in developing the pupils who are in school. It will not be enough to be able to measure how much or how many of these highly desirable ideals and characteristics each pupil secures in a given length of time; we must also be able to measure the exact part of the total which each teacher contributes.

Teacher Rating as a Salary Basis

The nearest approach yet made to a measurement of teaching ability is that of having each teacher rated by one or more supervisory officers. All of the arguments presented above prove to us that such a rating is almost purely subjective - a matter of personal opinion on the part of the person who does the rating. When such a rating of teachers is allowed to play even a small part in determining what a teacher's salary shall be, the natural feeling and knowledge on the part of all teachers who are rated low that the rating is personal and partial and unscientific more than offsets in loss of morale any possible gain which might otherwise attach to the use of this measure for administrative purposes. There is nothing inherent in the theory back of the single salary schedule which would prevent the incorporation of teacher rating as one of the bases to be used in determining salaries, but it is probably unwise, especially in a very large city, to incorporate this entirely subjective measure in any plan for the determination of teachers' salaries.

Lacking any objective measure for determining teaching efficiency, the Citizens' Committee was faced by the same problem that has had to be solved by every Board of Education - that of determining the best possible basis or combination of bases which may be accepted by the public and by the teachers themselves as an index or indication of this vague and unmeasurable quality called teaching efficiency or teaching ability. At the beginning of this chapter we have already recited a list of six or seven such indexes. We will discuss them here in some detail as to their possible sound use as indcators of teaching ability as the rating of teachers has already been discussed.

Salary Differentials Based on Sex of Teacher

It will be accepted without argument that the sex of the teacher bears no inherent relationship to that teacher's ability to teach. Undoubtedly certain teaching positions are best adapted to women teachers, and certain other teaching positions can best be filled by men, but there is no sound evidence that sex in itself bears a direct relationship to teaching ability. As society is at present organized the law of supply and demand does work in such a way that what seems to be the same quality of teaching service can be secured at a lower market price by employing women teachers. The Committee ruled out any such consideration at once, however, because the law of the State of New York requires that differences in salaries shall not be made on account of the sex of the public school teacher.

Age or Grade of Children Taught

One of the most controversial questions in the whole complicated problem of determining sound bases for teachers' salaries is that as to whether teachers of more advanced grades should receive salaries higher than teachers of equivalent qualifications who are teaching younger children. The precedent for higher salaries to teachers of more advanced grades has been well established and it is still the practice of the large majority of boards of education.

One defense for this traditional practice is that teaching older children is more difficult. Another is that it requires greater intelligence or a rarer type of teaching ability on the part of the teacher. Another defense is that it is a more important and valuable service to society. Another is that it requires more specific and extensive training.

The Board of Superintendents in the public schools of New York City have defended this practice on the grounds that the individual teacher should secure promotion in the system by beginning her teaching service in the primary school, preferably in the second grade, and, after some experience there, by qualifying for a license as a teacher of the seventh

to the ninth grades, this to be followed by a teaching position in the
senior high school. The license upon which teachers serve in grades
seven to nine is actually named a "promotion" license. It seems to be
the belief of the Board that second grade teaching is less difficult
than any other teaching position and that the inexperienced teacher
is more likely to succeed reasonably well in that position. It seems
to be the belief of the Board, also, that for a teacher to devote her
entire professional life to teaching in the primary grades would result in professional stagnation and lack of growth.

   All of the arguments here presented in defense of higher salaries for teachers of older children are balanced by arguments which
would lead one to conclude that this practice is entirely unsound and
undesirable. It may well be contended that no one teaching job is in
itself any harder than any other teaching job. For a teacher who enjoys working with young children, second grade teaching is undoubtedly
easier than teaching in high school would be. On the other hand, one
whose interest and liking is for children of high school age and whose
professional training is in the field of high school teaching would
find teaching in the primary grades very much more difficult than in
the higher grades. It is entirely true that faulty administration and
organization, either from lack of funds or for any other reason, may
make of the teaching of high school English, for instance, a matter
of dreary drudgery. If the teaching lead is such that countless hours

must be spent in reading and criticising theme papers, such work may be more difficult than teaching in the primary school even under the worst administration. That any teaching position is truly and intrinsically more difficult than any other teaching position is an argument most difficult to defend, however.

In like manner, it is difficult to defend the theory that the teaching of older children requires more intelligence or a combination of qualities more rarely found among teachers and that, therefore, the law of supply and demand justifies lower salaries to teachers of younger children. Such an argument might have had some weight thirty or forty years ago when primary and elementary education were largely formal and the teacher was in large measure a disciplinarian whose primary function was to force children to commit to memory certain facts and processes. In modern education, with our greater knowledge of the operation of the laws of learning, it is certainly true that no teacher requires greater intelligence or a rarer combination of desirable human qualities than does the primary and middle grades teacher. It is now accepted that each child differs from every other and that a thoroughly good teacher of primary children must be able to diagnose the strengths and weaknesses of each individual child if she is to adjust to him the sort of educational program which will make him develop so that he may "live most and serve best", as Dr. Jesse F. Williams has said.

So far as the Committee was able to discover there is no sound scientific evidence that the kinds of qualities or the degree of intelligence which make good high school teaching are any rarer than are the qualities and types of intelligence which characterize really good elementary teachers.

The defense of lower salaries for teachers of younger children on the ground that the service rendered by these teachers is less important and less valuable than that of other teachers must be accepted by any thinking person as entirely unsound and untrue. The exact opposite may well be argued. It is the elementary teachers who are teaching all of the children of all of our citizens who are patrons of public schools. Furthermore, they have responsibility for all these children when they are at the most plastic and impressionable age. On the other hand, a relatively large number of these children never enter high school at all. All of the education and training for citizenship which these pupils will ever receive in the public schools must be received at the hands of teachers of the elementary schools. To rate this service as less important or less valuable than that given in any other part of the public schools would be entirely absurd.

The fourth argument listed above is that teachers of older pupils require more extensive and specific training. This argument is of undoubted importance and significance. It is a fact that professional educators have not yet determined just what kinds and amounts of academic and professional training are most worth while for any given group of teachers. It may well be true that high school teachers may require two or three years of study and training at the college level in the subjects which they are to teach in high school plus the same amount of professional training which good elementary teachers need beyond high school graduation.

Until we have positive evidence, however, with respect to the most effective kind and amount of academic and professional training for any given group of teachers, we shall have no sound basis for paying higher salaries to teachers of older children for the sole reason that they have chosen or have been assigned to work with these older pupils.

The theory that teachers should serve an apprenticeship by practicing on the children of the primary grades and should consider an appointment to teach older children as a promotion must be based on the assumption that teaching in the primary and so-called grammar grades is unworthy to be considered as a profession in itself. The Citizens' Committee on Teachers' Salaries has no desire to put itself into a position so radical and absurd. It is the Committee's belief that any teacher whose natural likings and aptitudes are peculiarly adapted to teaching children of the second grade, for instance, will find all of the inspiration and satisfaction which she may crave in learning each year how to teach better and more artistically the pupils of the second grade. It is the opinion of the Committee that she will find all of the challenge to professional growth to which she can possibly react if she makes herself a student and practitioner of second grade teaching. The theory and practice of modern education are changing so rapidly that no worthwhile teacher can stagnate in her position simply because she is not forced to begin all over again and adapt her teaching techniques to the very different requirements of seventh grade or high school pupils.

Amount of Teaching Experience

Up to this point the discussion in this chapter has presented the arguments which were accepted by the Citizens' Committee in their decision that New York City teachers should not be paid on the basis of their rating by superior officers, on the basis of sex, or on the basis of the grade or type of school in which they teach. Two of the indexes which are commonly accepted as indications of teaching ability are yet to be discussed. These are (1) the number of years of teaching experience which the teacher has had and (2) the amount of professional or academic preparation which she has secured. Both of these were accepted by the Committee as valid and desirable indexes upon which to base teachers' salaries.

There are at least two sound arguments in favor of granting a teacher a certain number of yearly increases in salary for the sole reason that she has had an increasing number of years of teaching experience. In the first place, it is undoubtedly true that most teachers become better teachers with each successive year of experience for some years after they enter the teaching profession. A scientific study of this relationship between experience and teaching efficiency indicates that the maximum of teaching efficiency is most often reached after seven or eight years of teaching. It is entirely probable that most teachers who depend entirely upon their classroom experience to improve their teaching technique do not become better teachers after teaching for as much as ten years. The teacher who is a better teacher after twenty years of experience in the classroom than she was at the end of eight or nine years is almost certain to be one who has secured additional professional preparation during her teaching experience.

Kind and Amount of Professional Preparation

The second basis which the Committee accepted as a good indication of teaching efficiency was that of the amount of professional preparation which a teacher had secured. Practically every board of education and every thinking person accepts professional training as of genuine worth in improving teaching ability. The fact that every city board of education in the United States requires two or three years of training before a candidate is accepted as eligible to undertake teacher's examinations in order to qualify for appointment in the public schools is unanswerable argument in support of this universal belief. Candidates for positions as high school teachers are almost without exception required to have four years of training beyond high school graduation. In New York City those who would attempt to qualify for positions as elementary teachers must have three years of professional preparation beyond high school. The fact that this eligibility requirement has been changed very recently from two years to three years of training for elementary teachers indicates that the present board of education and Board of Superintendents accept professional preparation of a certain amount as absolutely indispensable to effective teaching service. Another indication of the general acceptance of the validity of this index of teaching ability is found in the fact that tax payers are allowing their representatives to appropriate annually millions of dollars of public money for the maintenance of state, county and city training schools for teachers.

The Citizens' Committee feels that its position is unassailable when it accepts the amount of professional preparation as an excellent index of teaching efficiency. It would be absurd to deny that there are individual teachers who have had no professional preparation at all who can teach better than other individuals may ever be able to teach even though they have four or five years of intensive preparation. In like manner, there are undoubtedly many individuals with two years of training beyond high school who are better teachers than are certain teachers who have had three years of training. But it must be remembered that the Committee was forced to accept the fact that there is not available any direct and objective measure of this intangible quality called ability or efficiency in teaching. The Committee faced the necessity, as stated above, of finding the best possible index or combination of indexes which would serve as an indirect indication of this most desirable quality or ability. Even though some teachers with two years of professional training teach better than do others with three years of training, it is undoubtedly true that the percentage of teachers with three years of training who will be really effective in their classroom work is decidedly greater than the percentage of effective teachers to be found among those with two years of training. That no teacher may now enter the New York City public schools without at least three years of professional preparation is sufficient evidence of the truth of this statement.

The Citizens' Committee has taken the next step, and an entirely logical one, in assuming that four years of training will make elementary teachers more effective than will the absolutely indispensable minimum of three years, and that five years of preparation after high school graduation will produce better high school teachers than will the required minimum of four years. The super-maximum feature of its proposed schedules is no more nor less than the Committee's method of expressing its belief in the truth of this statement.

Some of those who accept three or four years of preparation as an indispensable qualification for candidates for teaching positions tend to oppose any plan of paying teachers which would encourage them to do professional studying while in service as teachers. It is claimed that teachers who are taking courses desert the school building the instant the day's session comes to an end, - that their larger interest is in their professional studies rather than in their work as teachers. No evidence has yet been secured to show whether teachers who are doing professional studying leave their school buildings any more promptly than do those who are going shopping, or to the movies, or to afternoon social engagements.

The Committee attaches some importance to the claim that not all of the so-called professional courses are of practical value in the improvement of teaching. It also believes that teachers should be required to undertake and carry through well-balanced programs of professional study. For these reasons it proposes that super-maximum salaries shall be granted only to those who have secured the required amount of "approved" professional training. This recommendation implies that the Board of Education shall authorize some competent body - possibly the city board of examiners or the state department of education - to pass upon the kind and amount of training which will be accepted as of value.

Ability to Pass Teachers Examinations

The Committee, then, accepted the number of years of teaching experience and the amount and kind of professional preparation which a teacher had secured as two bases to be used in determining salary schedules. A third measure which it accepted without serious question was the ability of candidates for teaching positions to pass the sort of qualifying examinations which are set by the board of examiners. It was only indirectly that this measure entered into the consideration of the Citizens' Committee, since the Committee was concerned only with the recommendation of fair and equitable salaries for those already accepted as qualified teachers. The ability to qualify as a teacher - that is, to pass the examinations set for candidates - is, of course, a prerequisite for anyone who is to receive a salary as teacher.

Throughout its deliberations the Committee considered that it was not within its province to recommend policies to the Board of Education. Since the licensing of teachers is carried out in accordance with policies determined by the Board of Education, the Committee did not enter into that phase of the teacher problem.

At one stage of its deliberations it would have been entirely within its jurisdiction for the Committee to have recommended an extension of the use of examinations as a basis for determining salaries. This stage was reached when it was considering the proposal of a super-maximum salary for teachers of high professional status. The Committee recommended simply that teachers who qualified for super-maximum salaries should have one year of "approved" professional preparation beyond the minimum or standard requirements for their particular licenses. The Committee has left it to the Board of Education to determine what shall constitute "approved" professional preparation. It is entirely within the spirit of the Committee's recommendation that this approval should depend upon the ability to pass examinations upon the subject matter of the courses submitted for approval by the candidates for super-maximum salaries. The provision of such qualifying examinations would, of course, imply that the Board of Education did not care to accept at face value the professional credits granted by teacher training institutions.

The Number of Dependents or Size of Family

It is sometimes proposed that teachers who have many persons dependent upon their incomes should receive higher salaries than those who have a smaller number of dependents. This so-called "family wage" has been seriously considered for adoption by some boards of education, notably that of Mt. Vernon, New York. The idea seems to have been borrowed from southwestern Europe where some hundreds of thousands of miners are paid according to the number of children in their families.

It is the belief of the Citizens' Committee that the number of dependents which teachers have must be taken into consideration in determining salary schedules, but only to the extent that the uniform salary paid to all teachers with and without dependents shall be high enough that the indispensable teaching groups who have dependents may live comfortably and respectably.

To allow differentials in salary on account of varying numbers of dependents would most certainly defeat the very purpose which the proponents of this plan hope to achieve. It can be accepted that school costs are bound to increase if public education is to make notable progress. There is no sound reason for forecasting a lightening of the financial burden occasioned by the support of the public schools. Boards of education will be obliged to buy at the lowest possible market price the kind and amount of teaching service required. Under such conditions married men with children would find it increasingly difficult to secure employment in competition with young men and unmarried women who are equally well qualified to do the actual job of teaching.

The direct argument against the family wage is just as important. Teachers should be paid upon the basis of their teaching ability, measured as objectively as can be done, and not on the basis that boards of education are charitable institutions or are in some peculiar way to be held responsible for administering the State's obligation to provide for its own progress and perpetuity.

Educational Achievement of Pupils

Another indication of teaching ability or efficiency which is sometimes recommended as a basis for determining, at least in part, the amount of salary which a teacher should receive is that of the achievement of the pupils who are taught. This measure has the advantage of being entirely objective since it can be based on modern standardized tests whose scoring does not depend at all upon the personal opinion of the one who does the scoring. The Committee accepts it as true that no other indication of how well a teacher teaches is so objective as these measures of pupil achievement.

There are many reasons which caused the Committee to reject the use of such measures, objective though they are. In the first place, the administration of such a device would be most expensive. It would be necessary to give these standard tests to every pupil in every classroom at least once or twice each year. It would not be fair to measure the achievement of the pupils in only one subject, even so important a subject as reading, and to base a judgment of the teacher's efficiency upon that one measure. There would most certainly have to be given a battery of four or five tests, or one long and complicated test measuring achievement in four or five school subjects.

A second even greater objection is inherent in the present status of standardized tests in the field of education. While there are many excellent objective tests for reading, arithmetic and spelling and such drill or "tool" subjects, it is accepted by all authorities in education that there are not now available objective tests for measuring the intangible but most important products of public education such as ideals, attitudes, growth in character, and ability to appreciate the beautiful. The practical result of basing a teacher's salary upon the achievement of her pupils in fields which can be measured objectively would be that the sensible teacher would at once turn her whole energy to ceaseless drilling of her pupils and teaching them the kinds of facts and skills which can be measured. The Citizens' Committee did not care to accept responsibility for any such by-product of their recommendations with respect to teachers' salaries.

A third objection to basing teachers' salaries upon this or any other measure of pupil achievement or pupil status is the accepted fact that the teacher is not the only agency at work in educating the child. Each child is being educated at home and on the street and in all his contacts with all persons and things each day. No one has yet devised a method by which one may determine what part of a child's growth may fairly be credited to the school or to any one teacher. Still another difficulty is that one teacher's class may be much more able to achieve because they have been born brighter, or because they come from a neighborhood in which all of the community ideals exert an influence favorable to serious and painstaking school work. There are statistical devices to protect the teacher of dull children from being penalized because her children are dull, but the Committee knows of no device for protecting from injustice a teacher of bright pupils who come from a community in which high achievement in school work is not rated as an important mental and social asset.

Number of Hours of Teaching Service

It is seriously suggested by some that the number of hours per year which a teacher spends in the classroom should bear a direct relationship to the salary which she receives. Two applications have been made of this theory. One is to compare the salary received by a teacher with the salary or wages received by others the hours of whose working day are greater than the hours per day during which schools are actually in session, and whose working days per year are many more in number than are the days during which schools are in session. On the basis of such a comparison it is easy to appear to prove that the teacher's salary is much higher than the salary of corresponding groups of workers. Such a comparison is illogical and unfair unless it be frankly accepted that teaching is a part-time job, that the teacher has no professional duties which make demands upon her time outside of the hours when school is actually in session, and that she is free to turn to other gainful employment each evening, on Saturdays, and during the summer vacation.

The second application of this theory concerning the working hour of a teacher is that there should be a differential between the salaries of two teachers, if one of them has a longer school day than the other. If the Citizens' Committee had accepted this theory as sound, it would have recommended lower salaries for the teachers of kindergarten children than for teachers of sixth grade children since the younger children are in school a smaller number of hours each day. It is the Committee's belief, however, that any teaching position in the regular day schools is a full-time job, and that the recommendation of salaries based on the length of school sessions would imply that teachers are to punch time clocks like workers in factories and that they are to secure other employment for every hour of the working day when school is not actually in session. Whole-souled devotion to teaching as a public service would seem to be impossible under such conditions.

The Law of Supply and Demand

It is recommended by some that teachers' salaries be determined solely by the workings of the economic law of supply and demand. It is proposed that boards of education set up minimum qualifications for each type of educational position for which they have to provide, and that each board then go into the "market" and secure teachers who meet these qualifications at the lowest salary at which it can obtain the number of teachers needed. The theory of this position is unassailable. The Citizens' Committee accepts this theory in principle, but it is convinced that there are certain administrative safe-guards which must be provided in order to make it work in a practical way.

It is accepted, of course, that boards of education must establish minimum qualifications of such a kind that those candidates who meet the requirements will be thoroughly competent and efficient teachers. Having established such qualifications, a board of education is under the moral necessity of buying the kind and amount of service which it requires at the lowest possible figure. It is more immoral for such a board to waste public money than it is for an individual to squander his private fortune.

The determination of the administrative safeguards mentioned above at once leads one into controversial territory. The full acceptance of this economic principle could be interpreted to mean that those who were able to pass the examinations set by the Board of Education should then submit bids as to the annual salary which they would accept and that the Board of Education should appoint to each teaching position the person whose bid was lowest. Such an application of this economic principle would certainly be accepted by all as opposed to the public good. Under such a system teaching could never become a profession. The administrative safeguard which boards of education have been sensible enough to provide is that of establishing salaries at a level near that at which, in their judgment, they can supply their requirements, then to choose among those candidates who meet the minimum requirements those who are most outstanding, or those who most greatly exceed the absolute minimum established.

Another safeguard which the Committee deems it wise for boards of education to adopt is that of establishing salaries sufficiently high that those who are chosen for educational positions may live at such an economic and social level that they will be self-respecting and unharassed in meeting the necessary costs of comfortable and decent living. Even if a board of education could secure a sufficient number of teachers who meet its minimum professional qualifications who were willing to live in cheerless hall bedrooms, wear shabby clothing and subsist on the cheapest food, it certainly would be the poorest sort of economy even in the strictly financial sense. Such teachers could not bring their teaching up to the level of whole-souled devotion and enthusiasm which are too valuable to express in dollars and cents to those taxpayers and others whose children are under their instruction and leadership.

Another variation from a strict application of the law of supply and demand which must be accepted by boards of education in the State of New York has to do with the salaries paid to men and women teachers. No matter how high or how low the professional requirements be placed, it is possible under existing economic conditions to employ a woman teacher at a salary lower than that required to secure a man of equivalent qualifications. Because of this women teachers were for many years paid salaries lower than were paid to men. The social and professional effect of this strict application of the economic law was such that the legislature of the State of New York some years ago made it mandatory that men and women be paid equal salaries in corresponding educational positions. This was simply an acceptance by the representatives of the people of New York that the improved morale of the women teachers would be of sufficient value to justify the drawing up of this administrative safe-guard against the direct and unsympathetic operation of the law of supply and demand.

In summary, the discussion here presented has enumerated a great many bases which are proposed as valid for the determination of the amount of salary which a teacher should receive. It has presented the balancing of arguments which caused the Committee to discard many of them as unsound or impracticable, and to accept only three or four of them. Those which the Committee accepts are the following:

(1) The number of years of teaching experience,

(2) The amount and kind of academic and professional training,

(3) Under certain conditions, the ability of teachers to pass examinations set by the Board of Education, and

(4) The operation of the economic law of supply and demand, if it be so applied as to safeguard certain social and professional values.

B. CHARACTERISTICS OF THE PLAN ADOPTED

The plan of salary adjustment finally adopted by the Citizens' Committee was two-fold. All of the bases for determining salaries which were accepted by the Committee were combined into one plan. The Committee adopted this plan for recommendation to the Board of Education as the best method which could be used until such a time as there are objective measures of teaching efficiency which are acceptable to the public and to the teachers themselves. This recommended plan is not new nor unique. Variations of it are already in operation in many American cities. The name most commonly given to the plan is that of "Single Salary Schedule", although this name is inaccurate and misleading.

Under the operation of this system of paying salaries, no distinction is made between teachers of primary children and teachers of high school pupils, nor is there any distinction in salaries on account of the sex of the teacher. The different salary groups are determined solely on the basis of the amount of professional preparation which the teachers have secured. Under the present regulations of the Board of Education in New York City the lowest salary group would be those teachers who have three years of professional preparation beyond high school graduation. Since college entrance requirements and the regulations of state departments of education almost universally require high school teachers to have at least four years of training beyond high school, practically all of those in this three-year group would be elementary teachers.

The next higher salary group will be made up of teachers with four years of training beyond high school. In this group will be found all high school teachers who have only the minimum qualifications for high school teaching, and also such elementary teachers as have secured one year of professional training beyond the minimum requirement for their license. The teacher with four years of training who is assigned to kindergarten or to third grade will receive exactly the same salary as a high school teacher who has taught the same number of years. It will be noted that this plan is strictly in accord with the conclusions of the Committee as outlined earlier in this chapter. The plan accepts the teaching of primary and grammar grade children as of just as great importance and difficulty as the teaching of high school pupils, and that the well trained teacher of elementary pupils who has equivalent professional qualifications is rendering as valuable a service to the community as is the high school teacher.

Still another salary group will be those teachers who have the equivalent of five years of training beyond high school graduation. In this group should be found a small number of elementary teachers and a considerably larger percentage of high school and special teachers.

According to the figures given by the teachers in their confidential reports to the Citizens' Committee, approximately 78 per cent of the teachers of kindergarten to 6B grades would be placed in the lowest salary group; 13 per cent of them in the group with four years of training; and nine per cent in the highest salary group with five or more years of training. Teachers of junior high school and of grades seven to nine would have approximately 57 per cent of their number in the lowest salary group; 19 per cent in the middle group; and 24 per cent in the five-year group. A small percentage of the senior high school teachers would be placed in the lowest salary group because some of the teachers of vocational and trade subjects are not required to have the full four years of academic and professional training. At present this percentage of high school teachers would be 27. Twenty-four per cent of the senior high school teachers would be placed in the middle group; and 49 per cent in the highest salaried group.

It is conceivable that the Board of Education in adopting this plan for salary payment would create one other salary group for those teachers who have the doctor's degree, or the equivalent of six or more years of professional training beyond high school graduation. Some cities which are using an adaptation of this plan have created such a salary group. The Citizens' Committee is not in position to recommend that such a group be established in the New York City schools.

This plan adopted by the Citizens' Committee does not provide that all teachers in any one of these training groups shall receive exactly the same salary. There will be a minimum and maximum salary for each training group and a specified range of salaries between these limits. The minimum salary for three-year trained teachers, for instance, will be paid to those teachers with three years of training who have had no teaching experience, or who had had the minimum experience recognized by the Board of Education. The next year this teacher at the minimum would receive an increase in salary just as annual increments are now provided for each teaching group. This teacher would continue to receive a stated annual increment for a certain number of years until she arrived at the maximum salary for teachers with three years of training. But if at any time this teacher secured additional professional preparation sufficient to allow her to qualify as a teacher with four years of training, she would immediately leave the three-year schedule and begin to be paid according to the schedule for teachers with four years of training. She would not be placed at the minimum salary for the four-year group, of course, but at the salary indicated for teachers with four years of training who have had the same number of years of teaching experience as this teacher who is changing from one schedule to the other.

    The whole plan is pictured below in graphic and diagrammatic form. A beginning teacher may enter at the minimum salary for any one of the three groups according to the amount of professional preparation which she may have when she begins teaching. A teacher coming into the New York City schools from some other educational position may be placed at any step of any one of the three levels, according to her professional preparation and the number of years of teaching experience with which she is credited when entering the New York City schools. The salary amounts used in this diagram are for purposes of illustration only. As explained later, the Citizens' Committee did not consider it possible to recommend for immediate adoption this system of paying salaries and was, therefore, unwilling to recommend definite salaries which might or which might not be valid at the end of three or four years.

CHART 10

			5 yrs.	2400	2616	2832	3084	3336	3636	3996	4492	4936	5316
	4 yrs.		2040	2184	2340	2556	2796	3072	3492	3936	4392		
3 yrs.	1620	1752	1884	2064	2244	2496	2760	3060					

<u>Diagram Illustrating Proposed Plan for Salary Schedule</u>

(The three horizontal levels represent a schedule for teachers with three, four and five years respectively of professional preparation beyond high school graduation. The increasing amounts from left to right at each level represent the increases in salary with each additional year of teaching experience. Any teacher may move from a given salary level to the next higher level whenever she secures the additional professional preparation indicated.

The salary amounts written into the diagram are not significant. They are used only to illustrate the proposed plan.)

It has been stated that the plan recommended by the Citizens' Committee is two-fold. That part of it which has just been discussed and explained is the Committee's recommendation as to the ultimate solution of the teacher salary problem in New York City. Certain practical considerations caused the Committee to recommend that the adoption of this most ideal system be postposed for the present, but that the plan be put into operation not later than 1930.

There were two practical considerations which influenced the Committee in reaching this decision. The first, to which minor importance is attached, is the fact that many teachers and administrators are not familiar with the plan and are inclined to withhold their approval of it. While this is not an insuperable argument against its immediate adoption, the Citizens' Committee felt that it would be unwise to force upon the teachers a plan which they did not fully accept.

The second reason for recommending that this plan should not go into immediate operation was one of physical necessity. In order to administer such a plan the Board of Education must have available the facts concerning the professional qualifications of each teacher in its employ. It does not now have these facts. There is on file among the records of the Board of Education a statement concerning the professional training of each teacher at the time of her last appearance before the Board of Examiners. If a teacher has not taken an examination for a new license in the last twenty years these facts are, of course, twenty years old. It would be impossible to administer the salary plan proposed by the Committee on the basis of such records. It is the belief of the Committee that it would require two or three years for the Board of Education to work out a system of reporting and filing, to secure the facts concerning the present professional status of each teacher in the system, and to evaluate and appraise these facts for each individual teacher.

Having agreed upon a plan to be recommended as best adapted to secure equitable and fair salaries for all teachers, and having found it necessary to postpone for two or three years the adoption of this plan, the Committee faced the responsibility of making recommendations concerning salaries to be paid in the interim. The Committee felt that it was unfair to allow the present inequalities to continue until 1930, especially in the light of the evidence that certain groups have been grossly underpaid for many years. The Committee's solution of this problem was to recommend a "first step" in salary adjustment to be followed by the adoption, not later than 1930, of the salary plan outlined above.

Characteristics of the "First Step" Proposed

Since it is not now possible to re-group teachers in New York City according to their professional qualifications, the Committee was under the necessity of accepting the present classification of teachers into groups according to the license which they hold or according to the kind of educational position which they fill. It is therefore necessary for the Committee to recommend a readjustment of present schedules which will be more fair and equitable, but which will preserve in many particulars the characteristics of the present plan of paying teachers in New York City.

The distinguishing characteristics of the Committee's proposals for immediate adjustment of teachers salaries are as follows:

(1) It is recommended that the salaries of nearly all groups be increased;

(2) That all annual salaries shall be evenly divisible by twelve;

(3) That the first three or four annual increments of each schedule be small, to be followed by larger annual increments throughout the remainder of the schedule; and

(4) That a super-maximum salary be provided for those teachers whose professional preparation exceeds by one or more years the minimum requirements for license.

The first characteristic of the plan recommended for immediate adoption is entirely justified by the facts reported in Chapter III. It was there shown that practically all groups of teachers are receiving salaries with lower purchasing power than they received in 1910. Evidence was also presented in this chapter that present salaries are so low that teachers are finding it necessary to spend a disproportionate amount of their earnings upon food and rent. The amounts of the actual increases proposed will be found in Chapter VI.

The second characteristic of the first step of the Committee's proposed plan is of minor importance. Teachers in New York City are paid on a twelve-month basis. The Auditor of the Board of Education is authority for the statement that it would save thousands of dollars if the annual salaries are multiples of twelve. In that case the amount due each month will b> an even number of dollars, so the bookkeeping and writing of salary checks will be appreciably simplified.

The Committee proposes that beginning teachers shall receive small annual increments for three or four years. This recommendation is made because of the fact that there are many teachers who remain in the system only a short time. These teachers have no real interest in teaching as a profession, but are using it as a means of livelihood while preparing for another profession, or as a temporary source of income. It is the belief of the Committee that the greatest possible proportion of the total moneys available for teachers' salaries should be reserved for those who will make this type of public service their permanent professional interest.

The fourth characteristic of this proposed first step is one of very great importance. The super-maximum salary proposed by the Committee should be the forerunner of a new era in professional education in the City of New York. Heretofore it has been impossible to make any distinction in salary between the teacher who qualified for a position and made no effort to grow professionally and the teacher who was willing to sacrifice any reasonable amount of energy and money in order to keep herself alive in a professional way. At present the teacher who has taught for fifteen years and who knows nothing of the modern theory and practice of teaching receives just as much salary as the teacher who has kept herself in close touch with the great educational advancement which has been made in recent years. The Committee does not deny that a few rare individuals have kept themselves up-to-date professionally through private study and observation. Such individuals will be no worse off under the working of the proposed super-maximum plan than they now are. On the other hand, the Committee believes that any teacher who has secured as much as one year of professional preparation beyond the minimum requirement of the license which she holds will of necessity have a reasonable understanding of the meaning of modern education, and will be almost certain to be alive and up-to-date in her teaching. The proposed plan guarantees to these teachers a part of the recognition which they deserve. The Committee attaches even greater importance to this proposal because of the belief that it will stimulate professional activity on the part of teachers who have heretofore had no substantial incentive to improve themselves in service.

In each of the schedules recommended for teachers the Committee proposes that the super-maximum salary be reached through three annual increases beyond the regular maximum for teachers with only the standard or minimum requirements for each particular license.

The Committee has recommended one exception to the general rule that only teachers with an additional year of professional preparation shall advance beyond the regular maximum. In the case of teachers who have had thirty or more years of teaching experience it is proposed that two of the three super-maximum increases be paid regardless of the amount of professional training of these older teachers. This is a recognition by the Committee that it is impossible for the community to pay in cash the full debt which it owes to these teachers who have given a life-time of service to public education. Moreover the Committee recognizes the fact that it would not be humane and reasonable to require these teachers to undertake the physical and financial burden of securing additional professional credits.

It is suggested by the Committee that the Board of Education, if it is legally possible, adopt a ruling which will make it impossible for these older teachers to remain too long in service because of the large increase in salary which this recommendation of the Committee would guarantee them.

In summary, the Committee recommends for adoption a two-fold plan of salary adjustment. First, an immediate increase of the salaries of most of the teaching groups under a plan of payment not differing greatly from that in practice at present. Second, the adoption and putting into practice not later than 1930 of a plan of paying teachers solely on the basis of their professional qualifications as determined by the kind and amount of professional training which they have secured and the number of years of their teaching experience.

CHAPTER V

PROCEDURES USED IN DETERMINING SCHEDULES

In the preceding chapter it has been shown that the Citizens' Committee was forced to recommend two separate stages or steps in salary adjustment for New York City teachers. Because it seemed physically impossible to put into effect at once a plan of paying teachers on the basis of their professional qualifications only, the Committee has recommended that such a plan of payment be put into effect in New York City not later than 1930. It is the purpose of this chapter to explain in some detail the methods by which the recommendations as to the first step in adjustment were determined.

SUMMARY OF THE PRINCIPLES ACCEPTED

The guiding principles accepted for this stage of the Committee's work have already been outlined. It was agreed, for instance, that the principle of equal pay for the two sexes should be accepted, that the present plan of paying larger salaries to the teachers of older children should be continued in effect during this interim, that the annual increases in pay should be much smaller during the first three or four years of a teacher's service, that all annual salaries should be evenly divisible by twelve (12) in order to simplify the book-keeping in the offices of the Board of Education, and that superior professional training should be recognized by the payment of salaries higher than the regular maximum salaries for the teachers with only the standard qualifications for each license.

It was further agreed that immediate salary adjustments should give primary consideration to the relief of those economic groups of teachers whose living costs were highest, provided only that each group thus chosen as basic should be really indispensable to the successful carrying on of the type of schools in which it teaches. It was also accepted that such salaries should be paid to each of these economic groups that the average expense for food and rent should not exceed 55 per cent of their total annual salary.

It is stated in another section of this report (see page 43) that intensive studies of teacher budgets have been made in Michigan and California, and in a number of American cities. It has been found in these studies that the two items of food and rent most commonly constitute from 45 to 50 per cent of a teacher's annual expense. Since it is known that the cost of rent in New York City is disproportionately high, the Committee reasoned that it would be defensible to expect New York City teachers to spend as much as 55 per cent of their salaries for food and rent. If the Committee had accepted the more usual 50 per cent as the standard for New York City, it would have resulted in the recommendation of higher salaries. The acceptance of 55 per cent instead of 50 per cent is another instance of the Committee's conservatism.

It was agreed that the salaries of supervisory and administrative officers could not fairly be based on the actual expenditure of these groups for food and rent. The Committee therefore made a study of the relationship between the salaries of administrative and supervisory officers and the salaries of regular teachers in each of the large American cities from which it had secured the facts. The average of these relationships was accepted by the Committee as the best guide in establishing salaries to be recommended for administrators and supervisors. A more detailed explanation of this procedure is given on page 165 of this chapter.

In the final smoothing out and adjusting of the very many schedules which were to be proposed, the Committee did everything possible to avoid over-lapping of schedules which would result in paying supervisory groups smaller salaries than any considerable number of the teachers whom they supervised. Because of the complicated organization of the school system into elementary schools of both six grades and eight grades, the provision of junior high schools in some areas of the city and not in others and of senior high schools of both three and four grades, this over-lapping could not be entirely eliminated. For instance, in elementary schools of eight grades, teachers of seventh and eighth grade classes have to be paid on the junior high school teacher schedule. These schools are administered by elementary school principals and a part of the supervision of teachers is done by assistants to elementary principals. In order to recognize teachers of seventh and eighth grades of superior professional qualification, it was necessary to pay them a super-maximum salary which might be higher than the salary paid to assistants to elementary principals of less than four years of service in their positions.

The only possible method of preventing this over-lapping of salary schedules would have been a shortening of the range of each separate schedule so that the minimum and maximum salaries were much more nearly equal. This procedure would have made necessary either a very small number of annual increases in salary for each group, or a larger number of very small annual increments. Such a solution would have resulted in a leveling of the salaries within each teaching group which would have made impossible an adequate reward for years of teaching experience or for superior professional training. The Committee was convinced that such a plan would have been a great deal more undesirable than the occasional over-lapping of the maximum salaries of one teaching group upon the minimum salaries of a supervisory group.

ACTUAL DETERMINATION OF SCHEDULES

At this stage of its procedure the Committee had available the facts concerning teachers' salaries in other cities and concerning the present professional and economic status of New York City teachers. After a great deal of discussion and study the Committee had also agreed upon the principles which seemed most desirable as guides in its proposed schedule-making. It was now ready to undertake the actual determination of the salaries which it would propose for adoption during the interim preceeding 1930. In this section of the chapter the computation and determination of a number of these schedules will be presented. One of the simplest and easiest to understand is the schedule for senior high school teachers. It will be presented first.

Schedule for Senior High School Teachers

The first procedure of the Committee was to determine the economic group of senior high school teachers whose living cost was highest. This was an easy matter since all of the food and rent expenses of each group of teachers had been tabulated separately for the different economic sub-groups making up the total group. The Hollerith cards had been sorted by the electrical machines so that the statistical tables presented the distribution of expenditures for food and for rent for three groups of women high school teachers -- (1) those who were married and were living with their husband, (2) those who were unmarried but were living at home with parents, married sisters and so on, and (3) those who were living away from home and paying the full cost of their food and rent from their own earnings. The men high school teachers were divided into the same three groups except that married men were further sub-divided on the basis of the number of their children. It was thus possible to make a separate study of the living cost of married men who had no children, one child, two children, and so on to men who had the maximum number of nine children. These tabulations showed that the living cost of married men with children was higher than that of any other group of men or women teachers.

At this stage the Committee was faced by the necessity of deciding whether this group of married men teachers was indispensable to the successful carrying out of the senior high school educational program. All members of the Committee and all the educational authorities consulted were unanimous in agreeing that public high schools taught entirely by women teachers, no matter how efficient they were, could not possibly provide the sort of educational and cultural program demanded of these schools. It was agreed that there must be at least a small percentage of men teachers in these schools. If there must be men teachers, there must, of course, be married men with children. It is unthinkable that a man should be disqualified as a teacher because he marries and becomes a permanent and stable citizen of the community. There was, therefore, not a single opposing argument to the selection of married men with children as the basic group in the determination of senior high school salaries.

It is reported in Chapter III that 43 per cent of all the senior high school teachers in New York City are men and that three-fourths of these men are married. Seventy-seven per cent of these married men have one or more children. In other words, 25 per cent of the entire teaching group, men and women, are married men with children. At this point the Committee made a purely arbitrary decision to choose the married man with a wife and one child as the basic group instead of using the entire group of married men with children. This decision was made for the sole purpose of erring, if at all, on the side of conservatism - to avoid the recommendation of salary schedules higher than were absolutely necessary to a comfortable and decent living for married men teachers in New York City. Another reason for choosing the married man with children whose living expense was the minimum was to avoid increasing too greatly the differential between elementary and high school teachers.

It is true that 46 per cent of married men high school teachers have two or more children and fifty per cent of them have three or more persons who are chiefly dependent upon their income - that is, have a greater number of dependents than a wife and one child. In a later part of this section it will be shown that the basic group used in determining the salary for the elementary teachers was unmarried women living away from home. Seventy per cent of this group have one or more persons in addition to themselves chiefly dependent upon their incomes. As compared with this, 50 per cent of married men have a greater number of persons than a wife and one child dependent upon them.

These are the facts concerning the rent and food expense of married men teachers having a wife and one child: Half of them spend more and half of them less than $947 per year for rent and the middle figure on the annual expense for food was $1,222, a total average expense for food and rent of $2,169. As is shown in Chapter III, one-fourth of this same group spends more than $1,227 for rent and more than $1,465 for food for their families.

Since expense for food and rent was accepted by the Committee as the index or indication of the total need for annual income, and having reached the decision that food and rent should require not more than 55 per cent of this annual income, it was a simple arithmetic problem to compute the basic salary for senior high school teachers. This average expense for food and rent of $2,169 was divided by 55 per cent. The quotient was a little more than $3,900. This was accepted by the Committee as the basic annual salary for all high school teachers no matter whether they were women, unmarried men or married men with six or eight children. As has been stated in other sections of the report, the Committee accepted fully the principle of equal pay for the two sexes but refused to accept the principle of the family wage or a salary which should vary according to the number of persons who were dependent on the individual teacher.

In the schedule-making of the Committee the basic salary was not used as either the minimum or the maximum salary for any group. Instead, the schedules were so arranged that any group of teachers would arrive at a basic salary after five to eight years of service under that particular schedule. In the case of high school teachers it seemed reasonable to suppose that the typical man teacher begins his high school teaching as a young man before or soon after marriage and that he arrives at the economic status implied by the basic salary after four or five years of teaching. Again the Committee was conservative and arranged the schedule for high school teachers so that they would arrive at the basic salary at the end of eight years of teaching service.

Since the basic salary was used as a reference point, the decision that high school teachers should reach this salary after eight years of teaching had a very direct relationship to the minimum salary and to the amount of the annual increment which should be paid. Other considerations which were given weight in determining the minimum were the present minimum salaries paid to a given group of teachers and the minimum salaries proposed in the Rieca Bill which had been passed by the State Legislature and vetoed by the Governor.

From one point of view it is a defensible claim that the present minimum salary of $1,800 for high school teachers is high enough. It is known that persons who graduate from college rarely secure positions in business or in the professions which will give them a return of more than $1,800 to $2,000 the first year. The opinion is general, however, that present salaries and professional conditions are such that many of the most able and intelligent of college graduates are failing to be attracted into the teaching profession. It seems entirely justified to make minimum salaries sufficiently high that boards of education may secure the very highest type of college graduates for teaching positions.

As compared with the present practice of paying a minimum salary of $1,800 to beginning teachers in high school, the Ricca Bill had proposed $2,150 followed by two annual increments of $200 and then eight annual increments of $225. The Committee decided upon four beginning increments of $192 per year followed by six annual increments of $252.

It has been explained that schedules for teachers were established by computing a "basic" salary which was placed somewhere in the middle of the schedule and by using this basic salary as a reference point from which to work downward to the minimum and upward to the maximum salary. It is clear then that when the Committee decided that there should be four beginning increments of $192 per year followed by increments of $252 and that high school teachers should arrive at the basic salary after eight years of service, these two facts taken together established the minimum salary for that schedule. The minimum which resulted was $2,280.

It is the belief of the Citizens' Committee that so considerable an increase in the present minimum salary for high school teachers should attract to the examinations the very best of the graduates of colleges and universities. Under this proposed schedule a young man who enters high school teaching as a profession will receive $3,048 in his fifth year of service. Such a salary compares favorably with that which a young man might expect to receive in some other business or profession after he has been out of college four of five years. Under the present plan such a person receives only $2,400 during his fifth year of high school teaching. The Committee feels assured that the added expenditure made necessary by the beginning salaries which are recommended will yield much more than value received in terms of a higher percentage than now of the really outstanding young men who are going directly from college into business and the professions.

The maximum salary proposed by the Ricca Bill for senior high school teachers is $4,350. The schedule proposed by the Citizens' Committee establishes a regular maximum of $4,560. This maximum is reached at the end of the tenth year by all high school teachers who were able to pass the entering examinations and to secure appointment as regular teachers.

Those high school teachers who secure an additional year of professional preparation beyond the standard requirements for their license will receive three more annual increments of $252 after attaining the regular maximum of $4,560, thus arriving at the so-called super-maximum salary of $5,516. Fifteen per cent of the married men

with wife and one child are now paying for food and rent an amount
equal to 55 per cent of the super-maximum salary proposed.

One of the checks which the Committee used in determining the
reasonableness of each schedule recommended was that of comparing the
average salary which would be paid in the proposed schedule with the
average salary paid to the men teachers within each group in 1910.
This comparison was made in terms of relative purchasing power of
the dollar rather than in terms of the gross number of dollars received.

The comparison of salaries recommended for men and women
were compared with those actually paid to men only in 1910 for the
reason that the principle of equal pay for men and women was accepted
after 1910. It is the logical contention of women teachers that average salaries for men and women in 1910 may not fairly be compared with
the average salaries now paid since equal pay has become effective.

The average salary actually paid to men and women high
school teachers during the school year 1925-1926 was $3,293. If the
proportion of these teachers at each year remains the same in the
future as in 1925-1926 the proposed schedule would result in an
average salary of $4,229 the first year the Citizens' Committee
schedules were put into effect. In 1910 the average salary paid
to men high school teachers was $2,143. On the basis of the index
of the purchasing power of the dollar, as explained in Chapter III,

this average salary of $2,143 in 1910 would purchase as much as $4,322 in December, 1925. In other words, the proposed schedule for high school teachers would give them an average salary of only $4,229, $93 less than the purchasing power of the average salary paid to men in 1910. The Committee accepted this comparison as important evidence that the schedule proposed for high school teachers was fair and reasonable.

It should be kept in mind that the purchasing power of former salaries does not in any way enter into the determination of the schedules proposed by the Citizens' Committee. Such a comparison was used only as a validation of the schedule determined by the Committee through the procedure outlined in this chapter.

Schedule for Elementary School Teachers

The Committee followed exactly the same procedure in determining the schedule for the teachers of the grades from kindergarten to 6B as it employed in determining the high school schedule. In the case of these elementary teachers, the economic group whose living cost was highest was the women teachers who were not married and were living away from home, that is, those who were themselves paying the total cost of their food and rent. It was of course accepted by the Committee that women teachers were an indispensable group in elementary school teaching and that all women teachers should be paid enough that they could afford to pay cash for their own costs of living. The fact that married women and women living at home with parents or other relatives expended less for necessary living costs undoubtedly results from the fact that these women are in varying degrees the recipients of charity from their husbands or relatives. It would be indefensible to pay all elementary teachers smaller salaries because a large proportion of these women do not themselves bear the full expense of their own living costs.

One of the most difficult problems faced by the Committee was that of reaching a decision with respect to the employment of men as teachers in the first six grades of the school system. As was pointed out in Chapter III, only three per cent of all the elementary teachers of New York City are men, and a large proportion of these men are young college graduates with only two or three years of experience as elementary teachers. Because so many of these men are teaching under the beginning salaries of the present schedule their average salary is only $1,800 a year. Naturally their expenses for food and rent have to be very low. These expenses actually are lower than the corresponding expenses of women elementary teachers who are living away from home. Only a small percentage of these men are married. Few of them present any evidence that they are permanent members of the elementary teaching group.

If it were true that thirty or twenty or even ten per cent of all the elementary teachers in New York City should be men, the Citizens' Committee might have been justified in proposing for all elementary teachers a salary schedule high enough that married men with children could live comfortably on the salaries proposed. The fact that only or two years earlier than the high school teacher would reach her basic salary.

The present minimum salary paid to elementary teachers in New York City is $1,500. The Ricca Bill proposed a minimum of $1,600. The schedule adopted by the Citizens' Committee accepts $1,620 as the beginning salary, provides for three annual increments of $132, followed by three of $168 and those by three more annual increments of $180 each. The maximum salary to be reached by all elementary teachers who remain in the service ten years is $3,060. The schedule further provides that all elementary teachers who secure one year of approved professional training beyond the minimum requirement for their license shall be eligible for three more annual increments of $216 each. In other words elementary teachers who have an equivalent of four years of training beyond high school graduation will attain a super-maximum salary of $3,708.

The first proposal of the Committee was that the minimum, maximum and super-maximum salaries should be the same as are reported above but that there should be three increments of $120 and six of $180 each between the minimum salary of $1,620 and the regular maximum of $3,060. The present salary schedule provides for equal annual increments of $125. The Committee therefore ammended its first proposals so that no annual increment should be less than $125 in order to make sure that the adoption of the schedule recommended would not require action by the State Legislature.

In 1925-1926 the average salary paid to teachers of kindergarten to 6B was $2,433. The same distribution of these teachers upon the proposed schedule would give them an average salary of $2,639 the first year of the operation of the schedule, or an increase of $206 per year on the average. When the average salary resulting from the recommended schedule is compared in its purchasing power with the average salary paid to men elementary teachers in 1910, it is found to lack only $19 of having as great a purchasing power. The average salary of men elementary teachers in 1910 was $1,318. Applying the index of purchasing power (201.7) gives $2,658 as the average salary which would have been required December 1925 to purchase as much as the man elementary teacher could buy with his salary in 1910. It will be recalled that the schedule proposed for high school teachers lacks $93 of restoring to high school teachers the purchasing power of the man's salary of 1910. These comparisons were accepted by the Committee as important evidence of the validity and fairness of the two schedules.

An increase of $200 came nearer restoring the purchasing power of the man's salary in 1910 in the elementary school than did an increase of $900 in the case of high school teachers. This situation resulted from the fact that salaries of elementary teachers were increased much more, relatively, by the mandatory legislation between 1910 and 1926 than were the salaries of high school teachers.

Chapter III shows that the average salary of all elementary

three per cent of the elementary teachers are men and that very few of them are married men with children could well be a direct result of the payment of salaries which are too low to support men teachers with families.

The members of the Committee considered this problem of the desirability of men as elementary teachers from many angles. They reached the conclusion that at least during the interim preceding 1930, teaching in the kindergarten and in the first six grades of the public schools should be accepted as a woman's job.

Having reached the decision of considering teaching in the elementary schools as a position especially suited to the woman teacher, the Committee proceeded to the determination of the elementary teachers' schedule exactly as it had determined the senior high school schedule. The indispensable group whose living cost was highest was that of women living away from home. The average expense for meals reported by this group was $684 per year and the average rental was approximately $700 per year. This total of $1,384 was 55 per cent of $2,516. Two thousand five hundred and sixteen dollars was therefore accepted as the basic salary for all teachers of grades from kindergarten to 6B since the average expenditure of this group for food and rent would not exceed 55 per cent of that amount.

As in the case of the senior high school schedule, this basic salary of $2,500 was made neither the minimum nor the maximum salary but was placed within the schedule so that the elementary teacher would reach it at the end of six years of teaching service, teachers in 1926 had a purchasing power 133 per cent as great as the average salary of the same group in 1910. In the case of the high school teachers the average salary of 1926 was only 86 per cent as great in purchasing power as the average salary of 1910. A part of this difference is accounted for by the acceptance of equal pay for men and women. A larger proportion of women are found in the elementary schools than in the senior high schools.

Schedule for Junior High School and Grades 7 to 9

Attention has already been directed to the fact that the New York City public schools are organized into elementary schools of both six and eight grades and that junior high schools are provided for only a part of the seventh to ninth grade pupils. It has been the policy of the Board of Education to issue the same license to teachers of the 7th and 8th grade in eight-year elementary schools and to the teachers in the regular junior high schools. It is an interesting fact which throws light on the educational philosophy of the Board of Superintendents that this license for seventh and eighth grade teachers is called a "promotion" license. All of the teachers teaching under this license are paid on the same salary schedule. In keeping with this policy the Citizens' Committee has recommended the same schedule for teachers of junior high schools and of grades 7 to 9.

A careful study of the reports returned to the Committee by these teachers indicates that the group is made up of teachers with a wide range of professional qualifications. The junior high school is so new an institution that few normal schools and teachers colleges have trained any of their graduates for the specific position of junior high school teaching. In New York City, as in most other cities, the group is made up of senior high school teachers and of elementary school teachers who have been drawn from these respective schools and assigned to junior high school teaching. The wide variation in the qualifications of these teachers and the fact that the total group is really composed of two distinct bodies of teachers made it practically impossible for the Committee to work out a schedule on a basis comparable to that used for the senior high school and the elementary school schedules.

In nearly all cities which have different schedules for teachers of different types of schools, junior high school teachers are paid a salary greater than the elementary teachers and less than the salary of senior high school teachers. The Citizens' Committee followed this practice and has recommended a schedule whose annual increments and whose minimum and maximum salaries are about midway between the corresponding recommendations for the elementary and senior high school teachers. Because some cities make no distinction between the salaries of junior and senior high school teachers, because it was accepted by the Committee that a considerable percentage of the junior high school teachers should be married men with children, and because an increasingly large per cent of these teachers are required to have a minimum professional training of four years beyond high school graduation, the minimum, regular maximum and super-maximum salaries established for this group are a little nearer those established for senior high school than for elementary school teachers.

Accepting the facts and principles listed above the Citizens' Committee has recommended for these teachers a minimum salary of $1,980, and three annual increments of $156 followed by six increases of $252 per year. This results in a regular maximum of $3,960. As already explained in the case of the elementary and senior high school schedules, the Committee's recommendation provides for three more annual increments for those teachers of this group who have as much as one year of approved professional preparation beyond the regular qualification of four years of training beyond high school graduation. It is recommended that these three increments be of $252 each thus arriving at a super-maximum of $4,716.

It will be noted that the annual increments beyond the regular maximum salary in both the junior high school and the senior high school schedules is $252 and that the corresponding increases in the schedule proposed for elementary teachers are $216 per year. The Committee established this differential with two objects in mind; first, it was in accordance with their plan of establishing maximum salaries for junior high school teachers slightly nearer the corresponding recommendation for senior high school teachers than for elementary teachers; second, the additional professional training recognized in the case of the elementary school schedule is a fourth year of professional training beyond the standard three years required for that license, -- that is, for an additional year of under-graduate study. In both the junior and senior high school schedules, the super-maximum may be qualified for only by taking a year of post-graduate work beyond the standard qualification of four years of under-graduate training beyond high school graduation.

If the teachers of junior high schools and of grades 7 to 9 are arranged on the proposed schedule somewhat as they were on the schedule of 1925-1926 with respect to their years of teaching experience, their average salary would be increased $694 the first year the proposed schedule goes into operation. It will be recalled that the corresponding increase for elementary teachers was $206 and for senior high school teachers $936.

The average salary of the men who were teaching in grades 7 to 9 in 1910 was $1,850. At that date no junior high school had been established. According to the Committee's index of the purchasing power of the dollar, $1,850 in 1910 was equivalent to $3,731 in December, 1925. The proposed increase of $694 would result in an

average salary of about $3,800 for all the teachers of this group --
in other words would give to all these teachers a purchasing power
approximately $70 higher than the purchasing power of the average
salary of the men teachers of grades 7 to 9 in 1910.

Teachers of Atypical Children

At the present time no differential in salary is made between teachers of normal pupils and those who teach classes for the blind, for sight conservation, for deaf, crippled, tubercular and other atypical pupils. In the schedules proposed in the Ricca Bill the representatives of all the teacher organizations agreed that these special teachers should receive salaries higher than teachers of children who were normal. The Citizens' Committee likewise accepted the soundness of this point of view and recommended for these teachers a schedule slightly higher than that recommended for junior high school teachers.

The minimum salary proposed for these teachers is $2,100. The first three annual increments are $156 to be followed by six increases of $252 per year. The regular maximum salary proposed is therefore $4,080. The super-maximum for these teachers is $4,836 to be reached by three annual increments of $252 per year beyond the regular maximum salary.

It is the belief of the Citizens' Committee that the salary schedule for teachers doing this highly specialized and most important work in New York City should be sufficiently high to attract and reward teachers of special ability in these fields of teaching. Effective administration of these schools and classes will be made more easily possible and a supply of these well-trained specialized teachers should be much more likely to be available under the schedules proposed by the Committee.

Training School Teachers

One of the outstanding weaknesses of the present plan of paying teachers in New York City is that of making no distinction in salary between regular high school teachers and teachers in the training schools. As a result it has been very difficult to secure a sufficient number of good teachers for the teacher training institutions maintained by the Board of Education. The members of the Citizens' Committee were unanimous in the belief that a substantial differential should be provided for the teachers to whom are entrusted the vital work of preparing others to teach in the city school system.

Not only must the work of the training school teachers be highly specialized and adapted to pupils who are adults, but higher qualifications also are demanded of the training school teachers than of the regular high school teachers. No teacher is eligible for appointment in training school unless she has had five years of teaching experience, at least three of which have been in elementary schools. The regular high school teacher may qualify with a single year as a substitute teacher.

The schedule recommended by the Committee provides that the minimum salary for training school teachers shall be $2,400, $120 a year higher than the minimum for senior high school teachers. The proposed schedule also provides for ten annual increments of $264 and a regular maximum salary at the end of eleven years of service of $5,040. Those teachers who may have secured one year of approved professional training beyond the standard requirement for their license will then receive three more annual increments of $252, thus arriving at a super-maximum salary of $5,796. These maximum salaries are $480 per year higher than the salaries which may be attained by regular senior high school teachers.

It is the belief of the Committee that this substantial recognition of the peculiar importance and difficulty of the training school teacher's work should serve to solve the present problem of securing a sufficient number of well-trained instructors in the teacher-training institutions of the city. It seems that the Board of Education could expend public funds no more wisely and economically than in securing thoroughly competent and well-trained teachers for those persons who are to become the actual class room teachers of the boys and girls of the city.

Senior High School First Assistants

Under the terminology adopted in the New York City schools the regular class room teachers in senior high schools are called "assistants" and the heads of departments who have certain administrative and supervisory responsibilities for all of the teachers in a given field of subject matter in any one high school are called "first assistants". Some years before the World War these heads of departments were paid on a schedule approximately 25 per cent higher than that of the assistant teachers. This differential was decreased proportionately as mandatory legislation secured higher salaries for the New York City teachers until the maximum of $4,200 for first assistants was less than 14 per cent higher than the $3,700 maximum of the regular high school teachers. Since the position of first assistant is the logical and desirable promotion for the regular high school teacher it has been accepted by all those connected with the public high schools that the interests of all would be greatly advanced by restoring the proportional differential of the earlier salary schedules.

The Citizens' Committee has accepted the validity and desirability of this increased differential between the regular high school teachers and the heads of departments. It therefore recommends that senior high school first assistants shall receive a minimum salary of $5,700 followed by three annual increments of $300, thus arriving at $6,600 as the maximum salary for this position. The Committee thus establishes a maximum salary for this group approximately 25 per cent higher than the super-maximum for senior high school assistants. It, of course, does not recommend a super-maximum salary for first assistants. It is accepted by the Committee that any one who secures appointment as a first assistant will have professional preparation equivalent to at least five years training beyond high school graduation -- the qualification which is recognized by the payment of the super-maximum to the regular teachers.

Elementary School Principals

Up to this point this chapter has presented the application of the principles accepted by the Citizens' Committee in the determination of salary schedules for different teaching groups. The Committee determined the schedules which it recommends for supervisory and administrative positions on quite different bases. It will be recalled that the fundamental schedules for teachers recommended for the interim between the present time and 1930 gave direct consideration to the determination of salaries upon which the indispensable groups of teachers whose living costs were highest might live comfortably and decently in New York City.

The Committee has assumed that the social and professional demands upon those in supervisory and administrative positions may well require a financial outlay which bears a different relationship to the total income than in the case of class room teachers. It has therefore attempted to solve the problem of determining these schedules by attacking it from an entirely different angle.

It was recognized by the Committee that every Board of Education in the United States has faced and solved in some manner, haphazard or otherwise, the problem of the relationship between the salary of a principal and the salary of the regular teachers in his school. Expressed concretely and directly, the relationship between the average salary paid to elementary principals and to elementary teachers, for instance, in a given city, represents that community's evaluation of the relative economic importance of these two educational positions. The Committee reasoned that it could find no more valid basis for establishing the salary of principals than that of the combined judgment expressed in the most common practice in other large American cities. It is an interesting fact that in practically all of the cities studied intensively by the Committee the average salaries of elementary principals were almost exactly two times as great as the average salary of the regular elementary teachers.

Having established a schedule to be recommended for elementary teachers, the Committee then accepted this ratio of one to two as a basis in establishing a schedule for elementary principals. It is recommended that the beginning salary for this group shall be $5,064, followed by three annual increments of $360 each, arriving at a regular maximum of $6,144. It will be noted that this amount is almost exactly twice that of the regular maximum recommended for teachers of the kindergarten and the first six grades.

The Committee faced an embarrassing difficulty in attempting to establish an equitable schedule for all elementary principals. The analysis of the professional qualifications of these principals showed that their training ranged all the way from high school graduation to that of the equivalent of the degree of Doctor of Philosophy. The present requirement of three years training beyond high school for elementary teachers is comparatively recent. In earlier years many teachers began work in the elementary schools with a much smaller amount of professional training and some of them secured promotion to principalships. As a result, the present staff of elementary principals varies greatly in its ability to comprehend and put into effective practice the sound and valid principles and methods of modern educational procedure.

The Committee's solution of this problem was a recommendation of a super-maximum salary for elementary principals of outstanding professional training. This is the Committee's one exception to its policy of recommending super-maximum salaries for teachers only. In the case of these principals it recommends that those of the group who have the approved equivalent of six years of training beyond high school graduation shall receive three annual increments of $252 each beyond the regular maximum for the entire group of $6,144 -- in other words, those principals who can meet this qualification as to professional preparation shall receive a super-maximum salary of $6,900 per year.

It will be noted that the schedule for elementary principals establishes for all of this group a regular maximum salary substantially higher than that received by the highest paid group whose sole responsibility is teaching -- the training school teachers at a super-maximum of $5,796. The super-maximum salary for elementary principals likewise is established at a point $300 higher than the highest salary which the head of the department in senior high school may receive. On the basis of the index of the purchasing power of the dollar the regular maximum proposed by the Committee is 87 per cent as great as the maximum for elementary principals paid in 1910. The super-maximum salary proposed is 98 per cent of the purchasing power of the 1910 maximum.

Senior High School Principals

In 1910 high school principals in New York City were receiving $5,000 per year. This 1910 salary was a distinct reduction in purchasing power over the $5,000 salary paid them in 1900 since the cost of food -- and probably the entire cost of living -- had increased approximately one-third from 1900 to 1910. At the present time high school principals in this city are receiving only $6,500 per year or approximately 64 per cent as great purchasing power as they were paid sixteen years ago and less than one-half as much as they received in 1900.

The Committee's procedure in arriving at its proposed schedule for high school principals was the same as that outlined in the preceding section with respect to elementary school principals. The combined judgment of large American cities in establishing the relationship between the salaries of this group and the salaries of high school teachers and of elementary school principals was accepted as the most valid basis for determining the schedule to be proposed.

It is proposed that these principals shall receive a beginning salary of $9,000 followed by three increases of $600 each year, thus arriving at $10,800 as the maximum salary for the group.

The Committee feels entirely justified in recommending this increase of approximately 80 per cent in the present salary of high school principals. It accepts the fact, which is obvious to any one who investigates the situation, that this group along with the elementary principals and other administrative officers of the school system have been more or less the victims of salary legislation arrived at unscientifically as the result of mutual compromise among the several educational groups. The number of such positions available is small enough that the total increased cost to the city will not be large. The stimulating effect of the substantial salaries proposed should bear a very great indirect return among all of those in the lower salaried groups who think of appointment to such positions as the professional goal toward which they may bend every effort.

As was stated above, the proposed schedule restores to these principals almost exactly the purchasing power of the salaries of 1910 and approximately three-fourths of that of the salaries of 1900.

Junior High School Principals

Although there are many junior high schools in the New York city system, each with a principal in charge, the position of junior high school principal has never been established officially by the Board of Education. Technically the principals in charge of these schools are elementary school principals who receive a small bonus because they are assigned to the junior high schools.

The Citizens' Committee decided to limit its function to that of recommending salaries for educational positions as they now exist and to take no responsibility for recommending changes of policy to the Board of Education. In accordance with this decision, the Committee could make no recommendation with respect to salary schedules for junior high school principals since there are not at present any persons in the school system who are so designated.

It seems obvious to the Committee, however, that this position which exists in fact would very soon be created officially by the Board of Education. The Committee has therefore recommended that if and when the position of junior high school principal is established, the following schedule of salaries shall be paid to these principals: A beginning salary of $6,600 followed by three annual increments of $500 each, thus arriving at the maximum salary of $8,100.

As in the case of the other schedules for principals, the proposed schedule was determined on the basis of the relationship between the salaries of principals and teachers in the junior high schools of other cities.

Assistants to Elementary Principals

The determination of an equitable salary schedule for the assistants to elementary principals was one of the most difficult of the Committee's many complicated problems. These assistants combine the duties of clerks and supervisors of class room instruction. The superintendent of schools some months ago issued a letter to all elementary principals recommending that their assistants be given important responsibility in the work of supervision. The Committee has therefore recommended a schedule which guarantees to the lowest paid assistant a salary higher than the super-maximum received by teachers of kindergarten to the 6B grades.

Since many elementary schools are organized for eight grades, a number of the assistants to elementary principals have the responsibility of a supervisor of seventh and eighth grade teachers who are paid according to the junior high school teacher schedule. The schedule recommended for assistants provides a maximum higher than the highest salary which may be received by any 7th or 8th grade teacher. It was not practicable for the Committee to establish a minimum salary for assistants to elementary principals which would be higher than the super-maximum for junior high school teachers. To have done so would have resulted in a schedule with almost no difference between the minimum and maximum salaries, or else in a schedule which would have made it possible for an elementary principal to receive a smaller salary than that received by his assistant. It seemed to the Committee much less objectionable to provide for a slight over-lapping of the schedule for these assistants and for the super-maximum junior high school teachers than to have chosen one of these alternative plans.

The minimum salary proposed for assistants to elementary principals is $3,780. For each of four years following this first year the annual increase will be $240, the maximum salary of $4,740 being attained after five years of service.

Although the Committee recommends a super-maximum salary for both elementary teachers and elementary principals it makes no such recommendation with respect to assistants. These positions should be considered as a training school for future elementary principals rather than as life-time positions in themselves. Since there are almost as many principalships as there are assistants to principals, the chances of promotion should be most excellent. The Board of Education will undoubtedly find it much sounder professional practice to promote assistants to principalships than to promote good high school teachers to these important positions. In the first place, excellent teaching ability is no guarantee of fitness for administrative position and in the second place, the typical high school teacher knows little of the peculiar problems of elementary education.

Other Administrative and Supervisory Officers

In establishing salaries for the higher administrative and supervisory positions of the school system the Committee was guided by the same principles as it accepted in the determination of other schedules, but certain principles were accepted as of greater importance in this field of its deliberation than in others. It was agreed by the Committee, for instance, that the establishment of relatively high salaries for the highest administrative positions, while costing the city very little because there are so few of these positions, should yield a very great return in the stimulation to professional achievement which it would generate in the entire school system. In recommending these salaries the Committee assumes that these positions would be filled by those candidates whose merit and fitness for the particular position were most outstanding and that full publicity would be given to the considerations which guided the Board of Education in their selections. It is not enough that selections be made purely on the basis of merit and fitness for a given position; care must be taken that even the lowest-paid teacher in the whole system may know that each important position has been filled by the candidate of outstanding fitness for that position and that the selections are made for merit only.

The Committee recommends a salary of $25,000 for the superintendent of schools. This proposed salary is probably $10,000 higher than is paid in any other American city but it is not disproportionate as compared with $15,000 in Chicago with a school system only half so large, or of $12,000 in Philadelphia and Cleveland, and $12,500 in Detroit. If every teacher in the New York public schools knew that the superintendent of schools in New York City held that position because he has proved himself to be the ablest administrator in the United States, the Board of Education could well afford to pay an annual salary of $50,000 or more for this position of unique importance. It must be remembered that the position does not have the stability of tenure which characterizes many other administrative positions.

When one compares the salaries paid to the executive heads of industrial and business organizations whose administrative responsibilities bear no such direct relationship to the very heart and soul of our national life he does not find it a difficult matter to justify a proposal of $25,000 per year for the superintendent of schools in New York City.

The purchasing power of the proposed salary is only 25 per cent greater than that of the salary of the superintendent of schools in 1910.

In proposing salaries of $15,000 each for associate superintendents of schools the Committee was guided by the considerations outlined above and by the most common relationship between the salaries of the superintendent of schools and his associate superintendents in other American cities. Under the plan of administration in operation in New York City these men constitute with the superintendent of schools the Board of Superintendents, which is held responsible for the development of educational policy and the execution of policies adopted by the Board of Education. It is impossible to over-estimate the importance of these educational positions in the city school system, or the very great necessity that each of these positions be filled by an educator of outstanding fitness.

The Board of Examiners occupies a unique position among the administrative officials of the New York City schools. Its functions are largely judicial in nature. All of the arguments which are generally accepted in favor of the payment of large salaries to our federal, state and municipal judges apply with even greater weight to this position. Each member of this Board must be a man of known integrity and broad professional culture. No single function of administration bears a more direct relationship to the success or failure of public education in New York City.

The Committee recommends a salary of $13,800 for members of the Board of Examiners.

The district superintendents of the New York City public schools occupy a peculiar educational position. A sound plan of school administration would seem to demand that a district superintendent be the leader in supervision and the administrative representative of all types of schools within his particular area of the city. In actual practice the typical district superintendent is held responsible for the elementary schools only. It is true that two or three of these superintendents are assigned to high schools and to teacher training schools, but in general these positions are thought of as having responsibility for the elementary schools only. The result of this plan of organization has been that the district superintendents have been thought of as of equal rank with high school principals and have received exactly the same annual salary or, in recent years, $100 a year more than the high school principals. Because of this practice and the tradition which surrounds it, the Citizens' Committee revised its first tentative proposal of a salary of $12,600 for district superintendents and recommends that they be paid $11,100, a salary only $300 higher than the maximum for high school principals.

It is entirely possible that the Committee gave too much weight to the protestations of the district superintendents themselves, the high school principals, former members of the Board of Education and to members of the Citizens' Committee who were themselves in close touch with the public school system and its traditions. In any other city than New York it would seem to be true, certainly, that district superintendents should receive a salary greater than high school principals -- probably about half-way between the salary of high school principals and that of associate superintendents. It is entirely probable that even in New York the district superintendency will come to occupy that intermediate administrative position between the principals of all schools and the Board of Superintendents.

The proposed salary of $11,100 represents the Committee's attempt to retain the present nominal difference between the $6500 paid to high school principals and the $6,600 paid to district superintendents. It is a recognition of the present unusual relationship between district superintendents and high school principals and does not represent the Committee's ideal of sound educational administration.

The title of Director is used by the Board of Education to designate positions which vary widely in their importance and exercise of responsibility. One Director may have complete responsibility in enforcing compulsory attendance or may have complete charge of an important bureau such as that of reference and research. Another may be a Director of Sewing or a Director of the Art in high schools. The problem of recommending salaries for this type of position is further complicated by the fact that there are assistant directors, inspectors, assistant inspectors, supervisors, psychologists, and many other positions grouped within this same schedule -- Schedule No. 155 of the General School Fund.

It would have required an intensive survey of this whole field of "specific professional control" in order for the Committee to have made intelligent recommendations with respect to salaries.

After much discussion the Committee took action to request the Board of Education or the Board of Superintendents to classify this large group of diverse positions into whatever number of classes or grades they might consider desirable. With such a classification available it would then be possible for the Citizens' Committee to make recommendation with respect to a schedule of salaries for this group. At the time of the writing of this report the Committee is awaiting such action by the Board of Superintendents.

The schedule of salaries proposed for teacher clerks, library assistants, clerical and laboratory assistants and attendance officers are reported in the chapter immediately following this one. Small increases are proposed for teacher clerks and library assistants, but no change in salary is proposed for attendance officers and for clerical and laboratory assistants. These positions are more directly comparable to corresponding positions in business and in municipal administration and require salaries only high enough to meet effectively this competition. For instance, there would seem to be no defense for paying attendance officers a salary substantially higher than that received by a city policeman, or in paying clerical and laboratory assistants salaries high enough to secure applicants whose qualifications are higher than those needed for the successful carrying on of these positions. To illustrate again, it is probably indefensible to pay so high a salary to laboratory assistants that college graduates will apply for this position which is really intended to be that of a special janitor to care for apparatus in science laboratories of the high schools.

Schedules for Special Types of Schools

The Citizens' Committee recommends that the teachers in day vocational and trade schools shall be paid according to the schedule for senior high school assistants. This proposal gives these teachers a higher status than they are now accorded. The Committee has made this recommendation because two-thirds of the pupils in these schools are graduates of elementary schools and are therefore of senior high school level, both in age and in previous training. The Committee also wished to make it possible to transfer teachers back and forth from these schools to the industrial and trade departments of the regular senior high schools. Although the academic training of this group of teachers is lower than that of the regular senior high school assistants, the difference in academic training is fully compensated for by the requirement of practical experience and training of these teachers in trade and in industry.

The Committee also recommends that the teachers in parental and truant schools be paid according to the schedule for junior high school teachers and that the administrative officers of these schools and of the compulsory continuation schools be paid according to the corresponding junior high school schedules. It is proposed that the teachers in compulsory continuation schools be paid according to the schedule for the same grade of teaching in the regular schools. In other words a teacher of children of elementary grades in the continuation schools should be paid according to the elementary teacher schedule and a teacher of junior high school subjects in the continuation schools would be paid as a junior high school teacher.

It is not necessary to go into greater detail concerning the determination of these schedules for special schools. The Committee was guided throughout by the age and status of the pupils, by the instructional demands made upon the teachers and by the requirements of efficient, frictionless administration.

Per Diem Schedules

There is no occasion to go into great detail in explaining the Committee's method of arriving at the schedules recommended for those employees of the Board of Education who are paid a per diem wage. All of the evidence which the Committee could secure indicated that many of these teachers and supervisory officers are at present greatly underpaid. In general the recommendation of the Committee is for a considerable increase in the present schedules. Just as the Committee has recommended that day vocational and trade schools be placed at the senior high school level of salaries, it has also recommended that the teachers of evening trade schools be paid as much as the teachers in the evening high schools. The schedule for substitute teachers is made high enough that it will no longer be possible for the Board of Education to save money by temporarily filling vacancies in regular teaching positions by giving a substitute a regular assignment for a semester or a whole year to this position. At present it is possible to assign a substitute in the elementary school to a vacant position and allow her to carry the full teaching load for a whole year at the total salary of approximately $1,000 although the minimum salary which may be paid to a regular elementary teacher the first year of her employment is $1,500. The proposal of the Committee will make it just as inexpensive to appoint a regularly qualified teacher to such a position as to fill that position with a substitute teacher.

CHAPTER VI

THE PROPOSED SCHEDULES

It is the purpose of this chapter to present in concise form the schedules adopted by the Citizens' Committee on Teachers' Salaries and recommended for each teaching group. In the preceding chapter a number of these schedules are reported in connection with the discussion of the actual procedure used in determining them.

The schedules in effect at present in the New York City schools are here reported in parallel with the schedules recommended by the Committee. This arrangement should make it very easy to discover the significant facts concerning the Committee's recommendations: (1) The proposed schedules are, with few exceptions, higher than the schedules now in effect; (2) Each annual salary proposed is evenly divisible by 12: (3) In all of the schedules for teachers the annual increases proposed for the first three or four years of a teacher's experience are smaller than those recommended for later years of her teaching experience; (4) Super-maximum salaries are proposed for teachers in the regular day schools and for the principals of elementary schools.

SUMMARY OF PROPOSED SALARY SCHEDULES

A. SCHEDULES FOR TEACHERS IN REGULAR DAY SCHOOLS

Name of Group	Minimum Salary	Regular Annual Increments	Regular Maximum Salary	Additional Increments	Super-Maximum Salary
A. Kindergarten to 6B:					
Present Schedule	$1500	11 x $125	$2875	—	—
Proposed Schedule	$1620	(3 x $132) (3 x $168) (3 x $180)	$3060	3 x $216	$3708
B. Junior High School and Grades 7 – 9:					
Present Schedule	$1900	9 x $150	$3250	—	—
Proposed Schedule	$1980	(3 x $156) (6 x $252)	$3960	3 x $252	$4716
C. Senior High School Assistants:					
Present Schedule	$1900	12 x $150	$3700	—	—
Proposed Schedule	$2280	(4 x $192) (6 x $252)	$4560	3 x $252	$5316
D. Senior High School First Assistants:					
Present Schedule	$3200	5 x $200	$4200	—	—
Proposed Schedule	$3700	3 x $300	$6600	—	—
E. Teachers of Atypical Pupils:					
Present Schedule	—	—	—	—	—
Proposed Schedule	$2100	(3 x $156) (6 x $252)	$4080	3 x $252	$4856
F. Training School Teachers:					
Present Schedule	$1900	12 x $150	$3700	—	—
Proposed Schedule	$2400	10 x $264	$5040	3 x $252	$5796

The super-maximum for each of the groups listed above shall be paid to those teachers who have secured one year of approved professional preparation over and above the minimum professional training required of all teachers who take the examination for that particular license.

It will be noted that the Committee does not propose a super-maximum salary for senior high school first assistants.

B. SCHEDULES FOR PRINCIPALS AND OTHER ADMINISTRATIVE OFFICERS OF REGULAR DAY SCHOOLS

Name of Group	Minimum Salary	Regular Annual Increments	Regular Maximum Salary
G. Elementary Principals:			
Present Schedule	$3750	4 x $250	$4750
Proposed Schedule	$5064	3 x $360	$6144*
H. Junior High School Principals:			
Present Schedule	$3750	4 x $250	$4750
Proposed Schedule	$6600	3 x $500	$8100
I. Senior High School Principals:			
Present Schedule	$6500	None	$6500
Proposed Schedule	$9000	3 x $600	$10800
J. Assistant to Principal			
(a) Elementary:			
Present Schedule	$3400	2 x $100	$3600
Proposed Schedule	$3780	4 x $240	$4740
(b) Junior High School:			
Present Schedule	$3400	2 x $100	$3600
Proposed Schedule	$4080	3 x $240	$4800
K. Teacher Clerks:			
Present Schedule	$1200	7 x $100	$1900
Proposed Schedule	$1320	10 x $120	$2520
L. Clerical and Laboratory Assistants:			
Present Schedule	$1500	12 x $100	$2700
Proposed Schedule	-	-	-
M. Library Assistants:			
Present Schedule	$1700	10 x $100	$2700
Proposed Schedule	$1800	10 x $156	$3360

* It is recommended that elementary principals having six years of approved training beyond high school graduation shall receive a super-maximum salary of $6900 to be reached by three annual increments of $252 each beyond the regular maximum salary of $6144 for all elementary principals.

As explained in the preceding chapter the position of Junior high school principal has never been created officially by the Board of Education. The proposal of a schedule for junior high school principals and for assistants to junior high school principals is therefore contingent upon the establishment of these positions. The official action of the Citizens' Committee was to the effect that it recommended the adoption of these schedules "if and when the positions are established."

The Committee recommends that the salaries of the training school officials other than teachers shall be those proposed for the corresponding positions in the junior high schools.

The Committee makes no recommendation concerning a schedule for clerical and laboratory assistants in senior high schools. Analysis of the returns of the Committee's Inquiry Blank showed that a considerable proportion of those in this group were college graduates. Careful investigation by the Committee has shown that the relatively high salaries already paid to these assistants has attracted to the positions a group pf persons whose educational qualifications are higher than the positions warrant. The Committee therefore makes no recommendation with respect to this schedule.

C. SCHEDULES FOR POSITIONS IN SPECIAL SCHOOLS

N. Day Vocational and Trade Schools:
    Schedules same as Senior High School Schedules

O. Parental and Truant Schools:
    Schedules same as proposed for Junior High Schools

P. Compulsory Continuation Schools:
    Schedules same as those for holding corresponding licenses in regular day schools.

The Committee has accepted the function of Trade Schools as equivalent to senior high schools so far as the salary for these positions is concerned. In like manner it recognizes the parental and truant schools as on a par with junior high schools.

At the present time definite licenses and salary schedules have not been established for compulsory continuation schools. Administrative officers and teachers of these schools are assigned from other schools and are paid according to those schedules under which they worked before entering service in the continuation school.

The recommendation of the Citizens' Committee is that the present policy with respect to payment be continued and that teachers and administrative officers receive the new salaries proposed by the Committee for those of corresponding license. As in the case of junior high school principals, the Committee recommends that if and when these licenses for teachers and administrative officers of continuation schools are established by the Board of Education the holders of these licenses shall be paid according to the senior high school schedules recommended by the Committee.

D. SALARIES OF GENERAL ADMINISTRATIVE OFFICERS

	Present	Proposed
Q. Superintendent of Schools	$20,000	$25,000
R. Associate Superintendents	$ 8,250	$15,000
S. Examiners	$ 7,700	$13,800
T. District Superintendents	$ 6,600	$11,100

	Minimum Salary	Regular Annual Increments	Maximum Salary
U. Attendance Officers:			
Present Schedule	$1550	6 x $130	$2340
Proposed Schedule	—	—	—

The first four of the schedules presented above have been discussed in considerable detail in the preceding chapter on pages 172 to 177. It is not necessary to discuss them further in this chapter.

As is explained in the preceding chapter the Committee has postponed recommendations concerning a schedule of salaries for directors, assistant directors, inspectors, and the other officers who are listed under the general title of "Specific Professional Control" in Schedule No. 155 of the budget of the Board of Education.

The Committee does not feel that it is competent to make recommendations with respect to the salaries of the attendance officers. The duties of an attendance officers differ widely from those of the administrative, supervisory and teaching force of the public school system. The facts asked for on the Committee's Inquiry Blank were not such as to be of value in appraising the qualification of these officers. The establishment of a salary schedule for this group is a proper subject for a separate study by the Board of Education and the Mayor's Committee on Teachers' Salaries.

E. PER DIEM SCHEDULE

1. **Substitutes:**

    (a) <u>Elementary</u>

        Present Schedule $5.20 per day

        Proposed Schedule   ($6.00 per first 300 days
                                         ($8.00 per day thereafter

    (b) <u>Junior High School</u>

        Present Schedule $5.20 per day

        Proposed Schedule   ($8.00 per first 300 days
                                          ($10. per day thereafter

    (c) <u>Senior High School</u>

        Present Schedule $8.00 per day

        Proposed Schedule   ($10. per first 300 days
                                          ($12. per day thereafter

2. **Home Teachers of Crippled Children:**

        Present Schedule   —
        Proposed Schedule   ($9.00 per day first two years
                                          ($12. thereafter

3. **Evening Schools:**

    (a) <u>High Schools and Trade Schools</u>:

        Teachers:
            Present Schedule $6.50 per day
            Proposed Schedule $8.00 " "

        Assistants to Principals:
            Present Schedule $6.50 per day
            Proposed Schedule $9.00 " "

        Principals:
            Present Schedule $12.15 per day
            Proposed Schedule $14.00 " "

        Supervisors:
            Present Schedule $9.00 per day
            Proposed Schedule $10. " "

        Clerical Laboratory
        and Library Assistants:
            Present Schedule $3.90 per day
            Proposed Schedule $5.00 " "

E. PER DIEM SCHEDULES (continued)

(b) Elementary Schools

    Teachers, probationary
        Present Schedule $4.50 per day
        Proposed Schedule $5.00 " "

    Teachers, permanent:
        Present Schedule $5.50 per day
        Proposed Schedule $7.00 " "

    Teachers in charge,
    Fewer than 12 Classes:
        Present Schedule $5.20 per day
        Proposed Schedule $8.00 " "

    Teachers in charge,
    12 or more Classes:
        Present Schedule $6.50 per day
        Proposed Schedule $9.00 " "

    Principals and Supervisors:
        Present Schedule $7.80 per day
        Proposed Schedule $10. " "

    General Assistants,
    Probationary:
        Present Schedule   ---
        Proposed Schedule $5.00 per day

    Permanent:
        Present Schedule   ---
        Proposed Schedule $7.00 per day

4. Vacation Schools:

  (a) High Schools

    Teachers:
        Present Schedule $8.00 per day
        Proposed Schedule $10. " "

    Assistants to Principal:
        Present Schedule   ---
        Proposed Schedule $600 per summer session

    Principals:
        Present Schedule   ---
        Proposed Schedule $900 per summer session

    Clerical Assistants:
        Present Schedule   ---
        Proposed Schedule $6.00 per day

E. PER DIEM SCHEDULES (continued)

4. (b) <u>Elementary Schools</u>

    Teachers:
        Present Schedule $3.90 per day
        Proposed Schedule   ($6.00 first two years
                                    ($8.00 thereafter

    Assistants to Principal:
        Present Schedule   ---
        Proposed Schedule $9.00 per day

    Supervisors:
        Present Schedule $7.80 per day
        Proposed Schedule $14. " "

    Principals:
        Present Schedule $5.85 per day
        Proposed Schedule $10. " "

5. Community Centers and Vacation Playgrounds:

    Teachers:
        Present Schedule $3.25 per day
        Proposed Schedule   ($6.00 first two years
                                    ($8.00 thereafter

    Ass't Teachers, Librarians and Pianists:
        Present Schedule   ---
        Proposed Schedule $4.00 first two years
                                  $6.00 thereafter

    Substitutes:
        Present Schedule $1.95 per day
        Proposed Schedule $4.00 " "

    Supervisors:
        Present Schedule $7.80 per day
        Proposed Schedule $11. " "

    Principals:
        Present Schedule $5.20 per day
        Proposed Schedule $10. " "

6. Afternoon Athletic Centers

    Teachers:
        Present Schedule   ---
        Proposed Schedule $6.00 per day

    Supervisors:
        Present Schedule   ---
        Proposed Schedule $8.00 per day

7. Adult Classes in English and Citizenship:

    Proposed Schedule: Substitutes $4.00 per session
                                Temporary Teachers $4.50 per session
                                Permanent Teachers $5.50 per session

There is no occasion for lengthy discussion and explanation of the per diem schedules. In general the proposals of the Committee are for increased rates of pay. The Committee has attempted to make these schedules fair and equitable by studying carefully their relationships to the schedules proposed for full time teachers and the relationships of each per diem schedule to the other part time schedules.

It has already been pointed out that the proposed schedules for substitute teachers who have had more than 300 days of substitute teaching will give each substitute teacher who is assigned to full time teaching an amount approximately equal to the minimum salary for regular teachers.

The Committee has proposed schedules which place the evening trade school teachers on a par with the teachers of evening high schools. The considerations which influenced the Committee in this action are discussed fully in the section which relates to the proposed salaries for the day vocational and trade schools on page of this report.

It will be noted that section #7 of the per diem schedules for teachers of adult classes in English and Citizenship proposes rates of pay on the "per session" basis rather than so much per day. The explanation of this recommendation is, that since these classes meet at different hours during the day, some of these special teachers are able to teach two sessions per day. Others of course teach only one session. It is therefore impossible to pay them on the per diem basis as in the case of evening schools or vacation schools which have a single session per day. If one of these permanent teachers is assigned to two sessions per day for four days each week she can receive a maximum salary of $44.00.

COST OF THE PROPOSED SCHEDULES

In the case of practically every schedule reported in this chapter the Citizens' Committee has recommended a substantial increase. It stands to reason that increases of separate schedules most be accompanied by an increase in the total teacher salary budget of the city

New York City is at present expending approximately $87,000,000 per year for the salaries of teachers and administrative and supervisory officials in the public school system, regularly employed. The Auditor of the Board of Education has taken the schedules proposed by the Committee and has worked out an estimate of the increase in the salary budget which would be necessitated by the immediate adoption of the proposed schedules. This estimate could not be made with great exactness because of lack of authoritative information with respect to such elements as the amount of professional preparation which would be credited to individual teachers.

A part of the estimate is as accurate as could be expected in any financial forecast. This part has to do with the schedules for all teaching groups up to and including the regular maximum salary proposed by the Committee. That part of the Committee's schedules does not differ markedly from the present system of paying teachers except in the amount of the annual salaries proposed at the different yearly levels of the respective schedules. The Auditor's estimate of the increase in cost which would result from the adoption of this part of the Committee's recommendations is a total of $17,657,000. The detail of this estimate of increased cost is presented in Table II .

TABLE II

ESTIMATED COST FOR 1927 OF PROPOSED SCHEDULES
Exclusive of Super-maximum Feature
Prepared by Auditor of the Board of Education

	Number of Persons Year 1927	Estimated Cost of Citizens' Committee Schedules
General Professional Control	50	$ 245,700.00
Specific Professional Control	98	*
Principals of Elementary and Junior High Schools	419	627,736.00
Assistant Principals and Senior Teachers in Charge of Schools	23	7,294.00
Assistant Principals	651	738,760.00
Teacher-Clerks	736	352,900.00
Kindergarten – 6B Teachers	16,290	3,518,089.00
7A – 9B Teachers in Elementary Schools	2,854	1,773,946.00
Junior High School Teachers	2,186	1,276,526.00
Teachers of Atypical Children	753	561,664.00
Teachers of Special Subjects	980	601,048.00
Parental and Probationary Schools	19	12,714.00
Day High Schools	4,787	4,427,939.00
Training and Model Schools	212	307,980.00
Day Vocational and Trade Schools	198	161,555.00
Compulsory Continuation Schools	351	188,851.00
Visiting Teachers		*
Substitute Teachers in Elementary Schools	Variable	677,440.00
Substitute Teachers in High and Training Schools	"	215,220.00
Substitute Teachers in Vocational Schools	"	25,344.00
Home Teachers and afternoon Classes for Cripples	"	58,680.00
Teachers of Adults in English and Citizenship	"	38,000.00
Evening High and Trade Schools	"	265,888.00
Evening Elementary Schools Including Supervisors of Special Branches	"	176,000.00
Vacation Elementary and High Schools Including Summer Sessions of Institutional Classes	"	130,000.00
Community Centres and Playgrounds	"	130,000.00
Baths		
Afternoon Athletic Centres	"	150,000.00
Pupil Teachers	"	150,000.00
Attendance Officers	308	150,000.00
Administrative Civil Service Employees	1,500	150,000.00
Custodians, Elevator Operators, Firemen, Cleaners etc.	900	150,000.00
Estimated Cost for 1927 for Vacancies and New Positions to be organized between March 31st 1926 and December 31, 1927	2,512	988,000.00
TOTAL	34,807	$17,657,454.00

* No recommendation by Citizens' Salary Committee.

It is significant that the official estimate of the increase in the salary budget which would have been necessitated by the adoption of the schedules proposed in the Ricca-Strauss Bill - the bill drafted by the several teacher organizations and vetoed by Governor Smith -- would have been $18,823,000. In other words, the Ricca-Strauss Bill perpetuating or increasing many of the unfair discriminations existing in present schedules would have cost $1,166,000 more than the corresponding section of the recommendations of the Citizens' Committee.

It is explained in the preceding chapter that one of the most important recommendations of the Citizens' Committee is that of a super-maximum salary to be paid to teachers of outstanding professional preparation. It is impossible at this time for the Auditor or for any one else to make an authoritative estimate as to the increased cost which would result from the operation of this feature of the Committee's recommendations. It will be recalled that it is recommended that only those teachers should qualify for the super-maximum who have had one year of approved professional preparation beyond the standard minimum qualifications for the license which they hold. It is true that individual teachers reported to the Committee the amount and kind of professional preparation which each had secured, but there is no way of estimating what part of this training would be accepted for approval toward super-maximum salaries. The best guess that can be made from the evidence at present available is that the super-maximum feature of the Committee's recommendations would cost a little over two and a half millions of dollars, ($2,500,000) the first year of operation of the proposed schedules.

It will be remembered that only those teachers who are already at the maximum salary for each group will be eligible to qualify for the super-maximum. This estimate of $2,500,000 is based on the assumption that approximately 10 per cent of the elementary teachers who are now receiving the maximum, 40 per cent of the teachers of junior high schools and grades 7 to 9 and 50 per cent of the senior high school teachers who are at the maximum would be able to qualify for the first additional increment toward the super-maximum salary.

Twenty-two per cent of the women elementary teachers are now receiving the maximum salary of their schedule, $2,875. It is an accepted fact that the younger teachers who have not yet attained the maximum tend to have more years of professional training than do the older teachers. One explanation of this fact is that most of the older teachers qualified for their license when only two years of training beyond high school graduation were required. If only 22 per cent of this entire group, old and young, make claims to as much as four years of training beyond high school, it seems an entirely conservative estimate that less than 10 per cent of this older group who are at the maximum would be able to meet the qualifications set up for the super-maximum. It seems reasonable that the addition to this group of those teachers who have had thirty or more years of teaching experience would not raise the number above 10 per cent of those who are now at the maximum salary for elementary teachers. The same sort of reasoning was accepted in estimating the percentages of other teaching groups who would qualify for super-maximum salaries.

A consideration of all of the factors discussed above leads the Committee to accept twenty millions of dollars ($20,000,000) as the most reasonable estimate of the increase in the salary budget the first year the full recommendations of the Committee are put into operation.

The Citizens' Committee did not accept it as a part of their responsibility to make a careful study of the public funds available for increasing teachers' salaries. A number of members of the Citizens' Committee were also members of the Friedsam Commission, however, and other members of the Committee are thoroughly familiar with its fundamental study and its recommendations. The Committee wishes to go on record as endorsing the recommendations of the Friedsam Commission as embodied in the so-called Rice-Cole Bills providing for increased state aid to local school districts. These bills are now before the Legislature of the State of New York. It has been stated repeatedly in this report that justice to the teachers themselves as well as a consideration of the rights and needs of the school children of New

York City demand such increases in teachers' salaries as are proposed in this report, and the Committee accepts the provision of the Rice-Cole Bills as a sound and fair solution of the problem of securing the necessary funds for this purpose. It is estimated that putting the provisions of this bill into operation would yield to New York City an additional fifteen millions of dollars for school purposes the first year. This would make it necessary for the city government to provide not more than five millions of dollars beyond the present appropriation for school purposes. Since these state aid bills provide for increased payments to local school systems through three successive years, the bills are ideally suited to finance the increasing expenditure for teachers' salaries as those teachers who are qualified for the super-maximum become eligible for the second and third additional increments.

CHAPTER VII

THE COMMITTEE'S PUBLICITY AND OUTCOMES OF ITS STUDY.

The need of intelligent support for a public enterprise, such as that initiated by the Citizens' Committee on Teachers Salaries, gave rise to a publicity campaign. Publicity, in this sense, can be made to serve both the community and the organization behind it.

It was the aim of the Citizens' Committee so to direct its publicity policy not only that public backing might be gained but that an intelligent public opinion might be created, since without it but little can be accomplished. The Committee considered as part of its legitimate function the stimulating of this interest in a problem more vital to the community than any other - the securing of proper educational facilities for its children.

The committee set out, therefore, with the realization that the work of investigating the present status of teachers' pay and the making of constructive suggestions for its revision were but part of the service it might render the community. Fully as important a task was that of bringing forcibly and impressively to the public mind the need for an enlightened cooperation. Surveys, no matter how scientific and scholarly in method, are usually but of academic interest unless backed by the momentum of active public opinion. Such support enhances the possibilities of the committee's recommendations being utilized - translated into law. It was to insure this desirable end that a Publicity Committee was created. The publicity policy was carried out by the Committee's Executive Secretary.

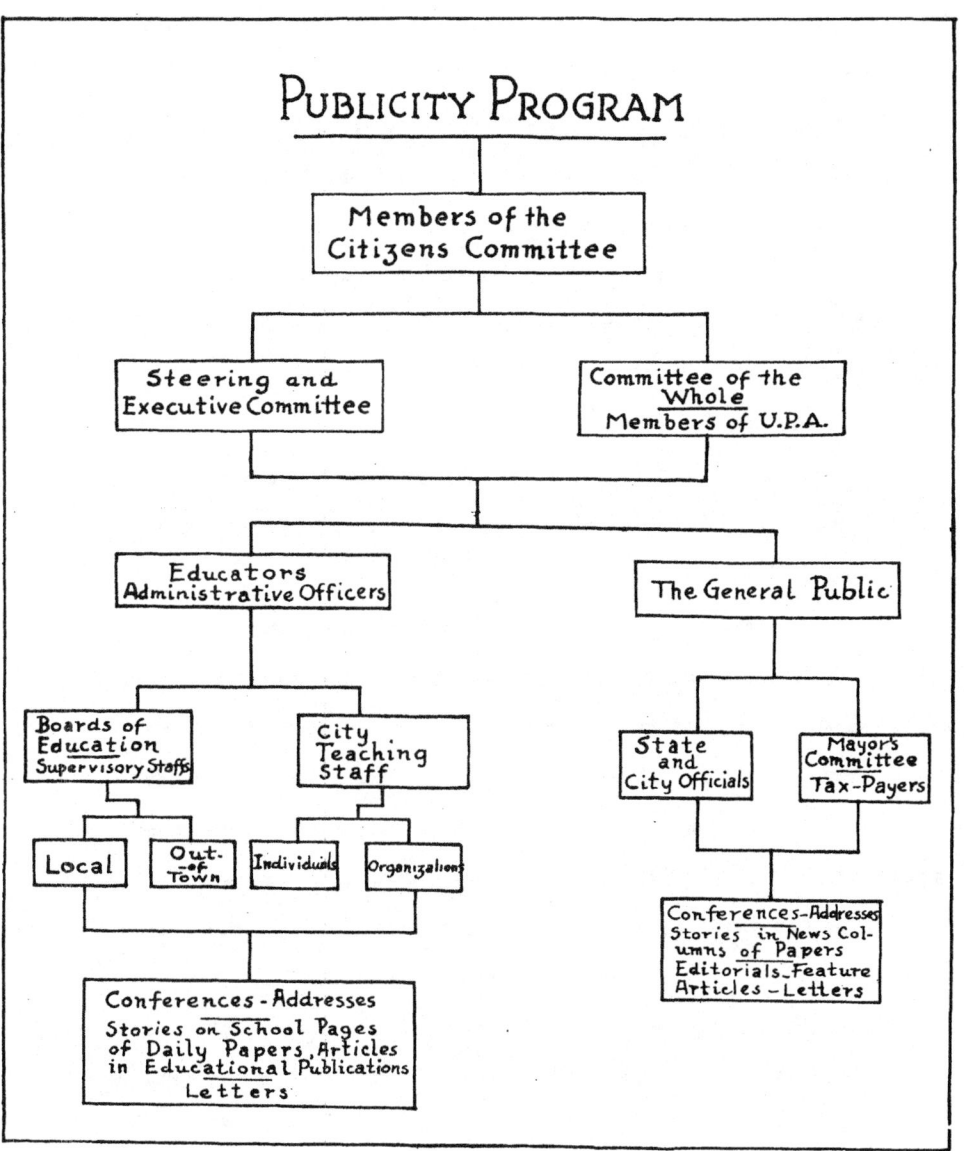

As a result of national publicity featuring the fundamental scope of the inquiry, many cities became interested in the organization of the Citizens' Committee. To such communities detail on the organization of the Committee may be of interest.

As a preliminary step most careful consideration was given to the proper and most effective organization of the Committee. Many conferences and talks with leading citizens gave rise to a concrete plan and a definite program of procedure. It was decided that the four elements absolutely essential to the success of such a committee were: (1) the selection of its Executive Committee, (2) the engaging of an expert of outstanding ability and reputation to conduct the survey, (3) the appointment of an Advisory Committee of Experts in economic and statistical surveys and (4) the appointment of an Executive Secretary to handle "contacts" and direct the publicity policy.

In the selection of its Executive Committee - the first step - much care was exercised that its personnel be representative of an impartial and non-partisan viewpoint. Only those individuals were urged to serve, therefore, whose back-ground of civic, social or educational interests was such as to inspire the confidence of tax-payer and the city's teaching force. To assure an impartial, unbiased attitude on this committee, no one remotely affiliated with the city's school system was invited to serve. It was thought that the chief contribution such a committee could make would rest on the fact that it was an entirely outside body. With these limitations on its membership in mind, the following citizens were chosen to serve on the

Executive Committee:

 Mrs. H. Edward Dreier, President of the Women's City Club
 Frederick H. Ecker, President of the New York State Chamber
  of Commerce
 Joseph P. Cotton, President of the Public Education Association
 Mrs. Seymour Barnard, President of the Parents League of
  Brooklyn
 Miss Martha Draper, Vice-President of Public Education
  Association
 E. W. Edwards, Chairman of the Committee of Education of
  the New York State Federation of Labor
 Dr. John H. Finley, Chairman of the Educational Committee of
  the New York State Chamber of Commerce
  and of the Merchants Association
 Dr. Lee K. Frankel, Vice-President of the Metropolitan Life
  Insurance Company
 George J. Hecht, Editor of "Children".
 Raymond V. Ingersoll, Impartial Chairman of the cloak, suit
  and skirt industries
 Ex-Senator Charles C. Lockwood
 John Martin, Ex-Member of New York City Board of Education
 Mrs. Henry Moskowitz, Member of Board of Directors, Women's
  City Club
 Mrs. George V. Mullan, Former member of the Board of Education
 Lawson Purdy, Secretary of the Charity Organization Society
 Nelson S. Spencer, Former President of the Men's City Club
 Mrs. Joseph Swan, Trustee of Teachers College, Columbia University.

The next step was the acquiring of an advisory committee. Four of the leading statisticians in the country agreed to serve in this capacity. The function of this Committee was to keep in touch with the progress of the Director's work, to advise the Committee, and, when called upon, to check up on the methods pursued in securing data. It was the Committee's good furtune that men of such outstanding ability as the following consented to give their valuable time to this important task:

Donald R. Belcher, Statistician, American Telephone and Telegraph Company.

Dr. Louis I. Dublin, Statistician, Metropolitan Life Insurance Company.

Professor Willford I. Kind, Economist, National Bureau of Economic Research, Inc.

Dr. Albert Shiels, Teachers College, Columbia University.

The third important decision to be made by the Committee involved the engaging of an expert to conduct the survey. With the concurrence of the Advisory Committee, Dr. J. R. McGaughy, Head of the Department of Elementary Education at Teachers College, Columbia University, was chosen. His unquestioned ability and notable achievements in the field of financial surveys had won national recognition. It was imperative that the man selected to act as Director of the investigation be an expert of outstanding reputation in whose statistical and scientific work both the Committee, the tax-paying public and the teachers might have confidence. Dr. McGaughy and the Executive Committee planned the scope of the survey. At each stage of the investigation Dr. McGaughy conferred with the Executive Committee in its five-fold attack on the problem. He was always available for addresses to the public and to the teachers for conferences with school administrators, local and out-of-town, and for personal interviews.

With the appointment of Miss Marinobel Smith as Executive Secretary, the fourth and one of the most important features of the Committee's organization policy was achieved. Much depended on the ability of the Executive Secretary to handle "contacts" and to direct the publicity campaign. To other cities contemplating the organization of a similar committee, a word might be said here of the manifold duties of such a committee's Executive Secretary. From the moment of its organization, the committee depends on this official to keep its own members, the city's educators and the general public constructively informed of its activities.

It is the function of the Secretary to keep in constant touch with members of the Steering and Executive Committees. The former committee consisted of five members chosen from the Executive Committee to carry on the more active work of the Committee. On all questions of committee policy and procedure, the Secretary must know when to call conferences and public meetings; when to arrange for interviews and conferences with the teachers and administrative officers of the school system, with civic and educational associations and with the general public. Through letters, personally written, this executive keeps other communities throughout the country advised of the Committee's progress.

Not the least service rendered by the Secretary is the conduct of a campaign for finances to run the Committee. But by far the most constructive and significant work done-without which the committee's survey could not have gained the confidence of public and educator - is that carried on under the title of "Publicity".

The Committee was most fortunate in having as its active chairman, a man whose life has been devoted to the promotion of educational welfare - to safe-guarding and seeing enhanced the quality of instruction received by the city's public school children. As the Committee's active executive, it was his duty to serve as its spokesman before public and private gatherings. As its official representative in the camps of friends and critics, it was the chairman's unflagging zeal that contributed no small part to its essential success.

THE PUBLICITY PROGRAM

In advertising parlance the business of selling the importance of teacher salary adjustment to an apathetic and in some instances an actively hostile public, was a "contract" beset with difficulties. It became necessary to satisfy the teaching and administrative staff that this was not just another of those surveys that investigated and investigated without getting anywhere.

For the benefit of the city's legislators, state and city officials and, when created, the members of the Mayor's Teachers' Salary Committee, all data giving a true and accurate picture of the economic and professional status of the city's teachers was accorded immediate publicity. A series of twenty articles presenting this information in detail was printed in New York City papers. (See page 204 for typical headlines).

Headlines Selected to Show Diversity of Story Appearing in Metropolitan Press

INFORMING THE COMMITTEE - THE FIRST STEP.

As indicated on the committee's publicity chart, the preliminary step in publicity taken by the Executive Secretary was acquainting the Committee's members with the nature of the survey. It was recognized that a committee of 120 representative citizens with their many affiliations can become, when properly organized, so many assets in the dissemination of information concerning the aims and accomplishments of the organization.

Each member of the Citizens' Committee was kept informed of the progress made, of the public's reaction and of the newspapers' support. This was achieved through informative letters, articles in the press, occasional meetings and individual conferences. Since many on its membership were affiliated with the United Parents Association, articles appearing in the "School Parent", the organ of that association, served as a direct appeal to member-interest. The following excerpt, for example, selected from this publication was the first of a series written by the committee's Executive Secretary:

"REPRESENTATIVE CITIZENS TO STUDY TEACHERS SALARY SITUATION HERE

Committee to Make Impartial Survey for Good of the Schools

    A representative non-partisan body of citizens has been organized to study thoroughly the whole problem of teachers' salaries and to recommend ways in which the community can improve school conditions. The group will be known as the "Citizens Committee on Teachers' Salaries," and may develop into a permanent advisory body having a broad interest in seeing that everything is done to help the teachers and schools to function effectively.

The United Parents' Associations of Greater New York Schools took the initiative in calling together representatives of a dozen of the leading civic organizations, who invited several hundred representative citizens to attend an organziation meeting, January 28th, at 8:30 P.M. at the Bar Association, and to serve.

Part of the letter of invitation reads:

> "Last year the Legislature passed a bill increasing teachers' salaries. The Governor vetoed the bill, suggesting it was a matter for local action. Subsequently the Board of Education voted an increase, but the Board of Estimate threw it out of the budget.
>
> "There are over a million children in the public schools of the City of New York, increasing, it is estimated, at the rate of 25,000 per annum. New and competent teachers must be found each year, not only for the additional children, but to replace those who leave the profession by death, disability, or resignation.
>
> "For the past six or eight years or more there has been a steady and pronounced decline in both the number and the quality of men teachers entering the schools."

Surely the teachers of our public school children, of our future employees, of our future neighbors and citizens, are entitled to a sympathetic interest and intelligent understanding on the part of every public-spirited citizen. Let us get at the facts impartially from the point of view of all concerned, - the children, the teachers, the Board of Education, and the City Administration.

It is proposed therefore that a large committee composed of public-spirited citizens, representatives of civic organizations, labor, representative employers, parents, educators, et al., be organized to ascertain the facts and to recommend such action as may be prompted by the findings. The aim is to secure a group that shall be representative of and function for the best interests of the City."

In keeping the committee alive and functioning, there were frequent conferences between the Executive and Steering Committees with the Director and the Chairman. At each stage of its investigations, the members of these smaller committees were called into conferences. In like manner the interest of the Advisory Committee of Experts was stimulated and retained through letters telling of the committee's activities, through frequent individual and group conferences. Since the purpose of this Advisory Committee, was to serve as a scientific check on all the committee's procedures, the importance of their constant and continuous interest was very great.

The business of handling this "contact" phase of the publicity compaign is an extremely important characteristic of any successfully organised committee. Properly and adequately executed, it makes for a smooth and efficient working organization. Such an intelligent and united front was absolutely necessary before the Committee could come forth into the broader arena seeking the respect and confidence of press and public.

THE COMMITTEE VS. THE PUBLIC SCHOOL TEACHER AND ADMINISTRATOR.

The importance and significance of a survey of teachers' salaries by disinterested citizens, as many editorial writers pointed out, lay in the fact that the study was being conducted by individuals outside of the school system. Its recommendations, therefore, would in all probability have more weight. Realizing the value in the eyes of the public and of the legislature of a thoroughly impartial and non-partisan attitude, the Committee did nothing to solicit the active cooperation of the city's educators in making its scientific survey. It did, on the other hand, make every effort to win the confidence of teachers. This was not easy. In the beginning there was an attutude both on the part of teachers and administrators that here was another stalling device - another superficial survey that would befog the issue of immediate salary revision and net the teachers nothing. These doubters - and there were many of them - had to be convinced of the Committee's sincerity and the scientific nature of the study comtemplated.

The motive behind the Committee's policy of constantly conferring with and informing the teachers of its procedures was simply to let them know they had a friend at court; a group of public-spirited citizens willing to defend their plea for increased salaries on it merits based on facts brought out by the investigation. At each stage of its operations, the Director conferred with the Joint Salary Committee which represented some sixty-odd teachers organizations. To bring about real harmony and understanding no step was taken without advising this body in advance. The result was the most hearty and enthusiastic cooperation when the Committee really needed such assistance. It manifested itself notably at the time the Director was ready to launch the 30,000 questionaires. The Joint Committee not only voted its approval of the questionaire but called upon all teachers in the system to cooperate with the Citizens Committee by answering it in full.

The story of how this early attitude of the teaching staff, one often of suspicion and resistance, gave way to such thorough cooperation is one of the interesting by-products of the Committee's work. It was accomplished through conferences, personal interviews, addresses to teacher groups, frequent publicity stories in the school pages of the papers and articles in educational journals. Impressed with the Committee's sincerity of purpose, this original attitude of indifference gave way to earnest cooperation. The Superintendent of the New York City School System, Dr. William J. O'Shea, wrote in a letter to the Committee's chairman:

> "May I close by repeating the expressions of appreciation and gratitude for the very important work which the Citizens' Committee on Teachers' Salaries is performing. The school system, the teachers and the supervisors, the parents, the children, are your debtors for your valuable and disinterested service."

Illustrative of the type of article that appeared in periodicals that reached the educator directly are the following excerpts:

School and Society July 1926

A PRELIMINARY REPORT OF THE NEW YORK CITIZENS' COMMITTEE ON TEACHERS' SALARIES

DATA drawn from more than 11,000 replies to questionnaires were presented recently in a preliminary report of the New York City Citizens Committee on Teachers' Salaries. The analysis was submitted to representatives of various teachers' organizations in the hall of the Board of Education by Dr. J. R. McGaughy, statistical expert of the committee.

Dr. McGaughy, as reported by the *Sun*, referred to the failure of a large number of teachers to answer the questionnaire. "These teachers did not know our personnel; perhaps they suspected our motives. I am glad, however, that we received a sufficiently large return to enable us to get a true picture of teachers' living conditions. This is one of the factors which surely enter into any scheme for the fixation of salaries."

Dr. McGaughy's summary was as follows:

The questionnaire classified all teachers into one of three groups as to their living conditions. In the first group there were those who were married and living with husband or wife. In the second group were those who were not married, but were living at home with father and mother, with married sister and so on. In the third group were those not living at home. These last were, of course, paying for their rent and meals on a strictly commercial basis.

It is interesting to note that this third group is largely made up of older women in the school system. More than one half of the women living thus have had more than twenty years of teaching experience. Unmarried women living at home average eight years of teaching and the unmarried man living at home has taught only four years. One half the married women teachers have been teaching fourteen years or more.

Interesting facts concerning the professional and academic training of the New York City teachers are presented in these tabulations. We find the typical woman elementary teacher has had two and one half years of training beyond high school. The men who are teaching in the elementary schools are largely young college graduates with little teaching experience, receiving an average salary of about $1,800 a year.

Junior- high-school teachers average a little less than the equivalent of four years of training above the high schools.

New York Teacher March 1926

The Citizens Committee on Salaries

The Citizens Committee on Teachers Salaries, brought into being by Mr. Robert Simon of the United Parents Association, E. E. Edwards of the New York State Federation of Labor and Miss Martha Lincoln Draper of the Women's City Club, is a wholesome sign indicating that the public has a definite responsibility in the maintenance of adequate living standards for teachers and in keeping them high enough to attract the finest types of men and women.

Regardless of the economic affiliations or background of the members of this committee, it must face the teacher salary problem largely from the viewpoint of the best interests of the cause of public education. The fundamental questions which they must face and answer are: (1) Were teachers adequately paid in 1900 or in 1914? (2) Does the 1926 dollar buy as much as the 1914 or 1900 dollar? If not, should not the teacher have his 1914 dollar returned to him in full? (3) If teachers are entitled to the restoration of their 1914 dollar, is it not the function of this Citizens Committee to use its influence to persuade city and state officials to do their duty with the utmost despatch and thoroughness?

In their efforts to secure adequate salaries for teachers the Citizens Committee will meet with the opposition of various realty groups such as the United Real Estate Association, which has opposed every effort to increase salaries, however necessary. They will even have to clash with groups like the Merchants' Association, which admits the justice of the teachers' cause but fights for "Home Rule," the application of which, experience has shown, will never result in securing increases for teachers. The third group they will have to encounter contains those who will say: "Yes, teachers are entitled to their 1914 dollar, but how are they going to get it?"

The test of the strength of the Citizens Committee will come when they face these objectors.

A resume of the Committee's activities appeared from time to time in educational journals of national circulation. The direct result of this phase of publicity - brought to the attention of the Committee through correspondence - was a country-wide endorsement of the enterprise. In a sense, the Citizens' Committee was establishing a precedent which other cities were desirous of following. Literally dozens of communities wrote the Committee, asking for guidance in solving their local teacher salary problems. So interested was the city of Chicago that a group of business men there started plans for a similar investigation of educational matters. William McAndrew, Superintendent of Schools in Chicago, wrote the Committee:

> "I do think this work is decidedly worthwhile. The idea of an impartial group of citizens attempting to determine the facts concerning such a matter as the salaries paid to teachers is absolutely sound. Such a report coming from outside the teaching profession would be impartial, and the general public would hav' much more confidence in it than one coming from the teachers themselves."

Another outstanding national educator, Herbert S. Weet, Superintendent of Schools in Rochester, New York, wrote:

> "Thank you cordially for sending me a copy of your report together with subsequent amendments. It all indicates the most thorough going piece of work that I have yet seen on this very important subject."

Similarly appreciative was the letter from E.W. Tiegs, Associate Superintendent of the Board of Education in Minneapolis, Minn. An excerpt from his letter follows:

"The work of your committee on teachers' salaries is of unusual significance. Not only is it the most comprehensive and authoritative study of salaries ever attempted, but the national discussion which it is provoking is bound to acquaint a great many laymen with the fundamental and vital nature of the contribution of education to the welfare of all other groups which compose our society. The personnel of your executive and supervisory committees should guarantee unquestioned acceptance of your results. I congratulate you on this notable achievement."

Interest in the survey was not confined to the United States. Among the interesting letters from foreign countries was a request for data on the New York study from the General Secretary of the London Teachers Association who wrote, "The information will be useful and valuable to the Committee of the Association". In all such correspondence, from whatever source, there is confirmation of the Committee's often repeated statement that this is the first time in the history of the country that so thorough and scientific a study has been made of teachers' salaries. There seems to be general agreement that in making such a study the Citizens Committee has contributed much to constructive educational research.

In explaining the Committee's publicity approach to state and city officials and the general public, too much emphasis cannot be placed on the value of the newspaper editorial. Constant publicity in the news columns of papers stimulates public interest but the editorial, written by an outsider, an intelligent and respected observer, serves that ineffable purpose of creating public opinion. When such editorial endorsement is unanimous, as was true in the case of the Citizens' Committee's study, not only the general public but public officials generally cannot help but be influenced. Examples of editorials that appeared in all the city's papers, commenting on the survey at certain critical stages in its progress, are here reproduced.

N.Y. Herald Tribune
Sept. 23, 1926.

Teachers' Salaries

The report of the Citizens' Committee on Teachers' Salaries has the outstanding merit of being based on fact, not surmise. The salary plan which it embraces, calling for increased pay for all teaching groups in the city's school system, is the outcome of six months' study of the situation by men competent and impartial who spared no pains to collect evidence and to weigh it.

When the Board of Estimate last spring asked Governor Smith to veto the Ricca bill and other salary bills it made the specific objection that the bills were not founded on a scientific or disinterested basis. The board resolved to appoint a committee of fifteen to make "a thorough and scientific study" of the entire question of teachers' salaries. That was a sensible step, but the committee has not been appointed. Exactly the work which it was to do has been done by the citizens' committee. The survey under the direction of Professor J. R. McGaughy, of Teachers College, with the assistance of several of the country's leading statisticians, is probably as sound a piece of work and certainly as fair minded as the city could hope to obtain from any source. The Board of Estimate has now a document of undoubted value to aid it in the salary adjustment which it has declined to make at random.

By means of questionnaires, to which 11,000 teachers replied, and by exhaustive study of salary schedules of the various groups with reference to the cost of living, the committee has attempted to work out basic salaries on which well trained teachers can live decently and comfortably. The increases proposed are not unduly liberal. They would give elementary teachers, for example, about 104 per cent purchasing power, compared with their 1910 dollar; junior high school teachers about 90 per cent; senior high school teachers between 85 and 90 per cent. The advances barely meet the needs of the teachers as judged by their ascertained economic status.

Substantial increases are recommended for executive and supervisory positions. Administrators, who carry the heaviest responsibilities, are at present relatively the most underpaid. This group is not large. It is decidedly in the city's interest to put no discouragement in the way of men and women highly qualified for administrative duty.

N.Y. Eve. Sun
Sept. 24. 1926.

Teachers' Salaries.

How to remunerate teachers of exceptional merit has always been a problem for those charged with the administration of the public schools. It is obviously impossible to let the department head in any civil service system fix the salaries of his subordinates—as is done in private employ—on the basis of his estimate of each individual's worth. The result is that so far as compensation is concerned every teacher is on a dead level with every other in his or her rank.

The Citizens Committee on Teachers Salaries hopes to improve this condition by a plan of "supermaximum" rates. Under the method proposed every teacher performing satisfactory service would receive an annual salary increment for a stated number of years until a "normal" maximum had been reached. For most teachers this would be attainable in the tenth year of service. From then on a "supermaximum" of $200 to $250 a year would be offered for three additional years to such teachers as possessed professional qualifications in excess of those required for appointment.

This may not be an ideal plan of compensation, but it is at least better than the present one, which rewards the conscientious and the indifferent in precisely the same way. It would provide recognition for the teacher with sufficient interest in his job to do post-graduate work. It would offer an incentive to others to get out of the rut of daily routine by attendance at summer sessions or evening courses. It should stimulate the entire teaching corps to become better acquainted with the latest developments in a profession which is constantly experimenting with new ideas and adapting them to the purposes of the classroom.

There is still another phase of the committee's plan which is commendable. Instead of providing equal salary increments for each year of service it would offer larger advances after the probationary period had been passed. This is on the principle that during the first few years after appointment the teacher is less valuable than when the theory of the training school has been supplemented by practical experience

Professor J. R. McGaughy, under whose direction the plan has been drawn up, and Robert E. Simon, who was largely responsible for the creation of the Citizens Committee, have done well to direct public attention to the principles which should underlie the determination of teachers' salaries.

N.Y. Times Sept. 23, 1926.

THE PAY OF TEACHERS.

While it is highly doubtful that the Board of Estimate will be disposed just now to vote more money for the salaries of teachers in the public schools, it ought at least to give serious study to the report on that subject of the Citizens' Committee. This is a document of uncommon force and merit, quite irrespective of the increased pay which it urges for certain classes of teachers. The Board of Estimate is temporarily in a panic about city expenses, and is permanently inclined to delay everything that can be delayed. But it cannot allege against the present plan the objections which were made to former proposals. They were opposed partly because they were regarded as unscientific, not to say haphazard. But the suggestions made by the Citizens' Committee are the result of careful investigation by authorities in education and by leading statisticians. Their report, whether immediately adopted or not, will furnish a model for other cities confronted by the same question, and will give the lead to all future discussions of teachers' salaries in New York.

Its boldness is seen in its plan to give only a slight increase of pay at the beginning to the largest number of teachers. But this is in order to prepare the way for increments of salary based upon experience and skill. Especially noteworthy is the idea of a "super-maximum salary" for teachers who deserve exceptional recognition for exceptional service and for additional professional studies which they have taken on voluntarily. It will be seen that one great object is not only to reward teachers who stay long and serve faithfully in the system, but to make the work and prospects so attractive that the existing large "turn-over" in the teaching force may be heavily cut down. This is certainly not only scientific but human-motive treatment. It is such qualities that make the report so important and full of promise for the future.

N.Y. Eve. Post Sept. 24, 1926.

It is faint praise to say that the Citizens' Committee on Teachers' Salaries has justified its creation. The report it has made is a model. It gathered its facts carefully, comprehensively and yet expeditiously; it adopted a scientific basis for its inferences and it proceeded to logical conclusions. If there are flaws in its recommendations, they are flaws of detail rather than of principle. The committee carries the idea of reward for preparation to new lengths by proposing a "super-maximum" salary for teachers who do extra work in professional courses. It also recognizes the claims of those who make teaching a permanent activity by reserving as large a part of the total salary budget as practicable for those who teach more than three years. These are sound positions and the committee is to be commended for taking them so emphatically. Actual increases recommended are smaller for teachers in the lower grades than for those in the higher, but the "super-maximum" salary proposed for even the lowest paid is an advance of nearly a third over the present maximum. The report merits the earnest attention of the Board of Estimate.

The problem of interesting the general public and the tax-payer in the importance of the investigation was brought about largely through a human interest slant given the Committee's publicity releases. Such publicity sought to bring to the heart and community conscience of the individual the necessity of his playing a cooperative role in the undertaking. It pictured, wherever possible, the gigantic size and complexity of the New York City school system - likened it to a city of a million inhabitants, administered by a force of 30,000 men and women, spending in a year over a hundred millions of the city's dollars for its up-keep.

The problem of managing such a city was emphasized as part of the public's business - the fair treatment of these educators and an investigation of their professional standing as the concern of the community. The pupils of today's public schools become the citizens of the metropolis ten years from now. It was constantly pointed out that a defect in the machinery of running this city of a million children. in any way responsible for getting a poor type of teacher or for the deterioration of a good type of teacher, was information which the community at large should know at once.

Newspapers treated all such releases generously. Publications of various civic and industrial concerns also gave space to this publicity. Probably the best summary of this phase of the Committee's publicity was contained in an article that appeared in the organ of the Public Education Association in the issue of January, 1926, from which the following excerpt is taken:

"The burden of deciding salary matters should not rest on the staff, but on the public whom it serves and by whom it is employed. For that reason the formation of this new committee is timely and essential. The committee's first job, as announced, will be to get at the facts. Its next and biggest job will be to weigh and marshall these facts effectively and to secure promptly the results they may warrant. The meeting for organization will be held on January 28th, at the Bar Association. Many facts are already at hand to begin on.

Sources For Facts

The teachers have drafted a salary measure, after two years's study by their Joint Salary Committee. This is based upon the Ricca bill of last year, which was passed by the Legislature only to be vetoed by the Governor, on the ground that salaries should be determined by the local authorities.

Following this veto, the Board of Education, after several months of study, drafted schedules which provided increases aggregating scarcely half of what the teachers requested in the Ricca bill. These schedules were rejected by the last Board of Estimate on the ground that the City was not able to finance them.

Thus the matter is again completely in the air. The burning question is, "Who is to do what?" The staff has been left high and dry, and , unless someone else acts intelligently in the matter, it will naturally go ahead on its own behalf.

Facing The Facts

The Citizens' Committee will at first find it necessary to appraise the data which underly the requests of the teachers and the supervisory staff, the proposals of the Board of Education and the contention of the City that it is unable to pay. It will then be necessary for it to determine what is just and possible and to what extent the cost involved must be shared by the State and the City. Legislation will be necessary whatever the decision, and that makes promptness imperative.

Evidently there is not only a big task ahead, but a splendid opportunity for everyone to face the facts and work for a disinterested judgment. There will doubtless be on this committee men of affairs who are either employers of large staffs or representatives of great labor organizations. If they will apply to this public task the same insight they use in their private affairs, they can lead the way to a practical and satisfactory solution."

No picture of the Committee's survey is representative and true which does not present both the favorable and adverse criticism that greeted publication of its salary recommendations. It was but natural and to be expected that some groups of teachers would be dissatisfied. No bills prepared by the teachers had succeeded in getting the unqualified support of all teaching groups. Even the Ricca Bill which had such general backing from the rank and file had failed to conciliate several groups within the system. Any set of salary schedules, prepared for so huge and complex a group as the city's 30,000 educators, is bound to work what seem to be injustices for some individuals within the separate groups.

The reaction on the part of some of the elementary teachers who felt discriminated against in the revised schedules was immediate and emphatic. Briefs were submitted calling on the Committee to revise the schedules for this group of teachers, and citing specific reasons and arguments in favor of such changes. The Executive Committee answered this brief, point by point, showing the economic soundness of its procedures in arriving at the proposed schedules. The answer did not satisfy these elementary teachers and the controversy was carried to the press. (The full text of the committee's reply to the brief submitted by the elementary teachers is incorporated in an article that appeared in the New York Evening Sun, October 20, 1926. An excerpt of this may be found on Page 222B).

Briefs from several other groups of teachers voicing similar grievances were submitted and, after careful consideration by the Executive Committee, they were answered. With but one exception, the Committee endeavored to meet and answer the criticisms of teachers and individuals outside of the teaching system, either through newspaper publicity conferences, or by correspondence. The exception noted was the case of an individual in whose sincerity and open-mindedness, because of gross misstatements made in the press, the Committee's executive board had little confidence.

THE MAYORS COMMISSION ON TEACHERS' SALARIES

With the appointment of an official committee to investigate teachers' salaries, authorized by a resolution passed by the Board of Estimate and Apportionment and created by Mayor Walker, October 10, 1926, teacher salary publicity entered a new phase. The chairman of the Citizens' Committee immediately wrote to Mr. Lincoln Cromwell, the chairman of the Mayor's Committee and offered all the data compiled by the Citizens' Committee. By establishing the policy of giving hearings to representatives of all the teachers' organizations, this group of fifteen citizens, known as the Mayor's Committee on Teachers' Salaries, kept the Citizens' Committee's report daily before the public. The hearings gave all groups in the school system an excellent opportunity to voice their respective grievances or endorsements of the Committee's plan and schedules.

There was no feature of the plan suggested by the Citizens' Committee which did not come in for praise or blame in the hearings before this body. Time and again the chairman of the Mayor's Committee would ask the representative of a teaching group what he or she thought of the Citizens' Committee's schedules, of the single salary plan, or of the super-maximum feature. The question invariably led to a discussion based on the Committee's report. The single salary schedule was commended as the most forward-looking step in years - it was denounced as a piece of idealistic tom-foolery that would lead to lower salaries for all teachers. The super-maximum salary was praised as a device to insure better-prepared teachers in all groups - it was arraigned as a scheme that paid teachers for credits rather than for service. The schedules recommended were unfair and discriminatory - they were fair and equitable. (See page 222A for typical headlines showing the diversity of reaction to the committee's plan and schedules.)

In view of the fact that teachers felt at perfect liberty to express themselves at these hearings, free to criticize or to endorse, one gets a fairly accurate estimate of teacher sentiment concerning the salary plan recommended by the Citizens' Committee from the minutes of these hearings before the Mayor's Committee. These minutes reveal an almost unanimous endorsement of these schedules with occasional enthusiastic espousal of the single salary plan and the super-maximum provision of the "first step" proposed. The minutes show that the largest dissatisfied group - the elementary teachers - were not themselves unanimous in opposing the schedules; two of the groups representing their interests having endorsed both the schedules and the single salary plan. The teacher groups endorsing the schedules recommended by the Citizens' Committee number some fifty-three associations.

One of the motivating reasons which actuated the Committee in undertaking this work was to try and raise the morale of the teaching staff, as well as to see that justice and equity were being done in the schedules of salaries. That the former of these objectives was accomplished was evidenced by the fact that for the first time in the history of the city there had been a plan of salaries around which the teachers could rally, and upon which they could base their recommendations and requests. It was a source of great satisfaction to the members of the Citizens' Committee to see the attitude of the individuals who formerly appeared before the State Legislature clamoring for their rights, intimidating, and using the methods of politicians, changed to an attitude of perfect frankness and a desire to enlighten the members of the Mayor's Committee and aid them in their search for a sound and sane solution of this very vexing problem.

The Committee has on file scores of letters from individual teachers and teachers' organizations expressing appreciation of the work done in their behalf. An even more significant evidence of teacher appreciation is seen from a summary study of selected headlines and captions appearing on page 222A, taken from New York papers that covered the hearings before the Mayor's Salary Commission. The Committee's executives, themselves, were pleasantly surprised at the enthusiastic and general acceptance of the schedules and plan it recommended for salary adjustment. The correspondence here reproduced indicates the general tone of such teacher appreciation and endorsement:

> "The undersigned committee, acting for the Association of First Asst. Teachers in High and Training Schools, beg to express to you, and through you, to your committee, their deep appreciation of your untiring efforts to prepare a scientific and equitable set of salary schedules for teachers.
>
> While it would be humanly impossible to secure the unqualified approval of every teacher, you may be assured that the undersigned committee are ready to extend to you their solid support of the schedules you have recommended, and wish to be placed on record as endorsing your report.
>
> The committee are unanimous in believing that the salaries you propose are equitable, and they hope that you will be successful in securing favorable action by the city authorities in time to put the schedules into effect on Jan. 1, 1927."

Selected Captions Showing Teacher-Reaction to C.C. Report

WOMEN APPROVE CITIZENS' RATES

Ask All Other Teachers to Support Plan.

TEACHERS BURY DIFFERENCES ON PAY SCHEDULES

To Unite in Campaign, Using Citizens' Report to Justify Claims.

WILL SEEK ALBANY ACT

Plan of Mayor's Committee Not Satisfactory, Will Offer Own Bill.

JUNIOR HIGH CORPS BACKS PAY PLAN

Asks Support for Citizens Committee Rates.

FEDERATION OF TEACHERS HITS 'SINGLE SALARY'

Will Mean Lowering of Rates, Asserts Organization — Own Plan.

INDORSE SALARY PLAN, BUT NOT SUPER-MAXIMUM

Upper Grade Teachers View Extra Bonus as Detriment

URGE SINGLE PAY IDEA

Elementary Teachers Back Citizens' Report.

GRADE TEACHERS PROTEST STATUS

Say Citizens' Pay Rate Will Lower Standards.

SEE 'FOUNDATION' ENDANGERED

Want Experienced Instructors in Lower Classes.

PRINCIPALS BACK CITIZENS' SURVEY

Indorse Report, but With 'Certain Adjustments.'

TWO SCHOOLS OUT FOR CITIZENS' PLAN

Jefferson and Clinton High Faculties Act.

BACK CITIZENS' RATES

New York City Teachers Approve Features of Report.

SUBSTITUTES INDORSE

Approve Rates Contained in Citizens' Report.

FIRST ASSISTANTS ACT

Appove the Salary Plan of the Citizens Committee.

1910 VALUE OF TEACHER'S PAY IN NEW PLAN

One of the chief grievances expressed by the kindergarten to 6B teachers was that the citizens' plan failed to restore to the elementary teachers' group the purchasing power which the men teachers in the elementary schools enjoyed in 1910. According to figures submitted by the committee, however, the average rate it has recommended for the elementary group comes withing $19 of the figures calculated as necessary to restore the 1910 value of their dollar. This is a much closer approximation than in the case of the high school schedule.

"The average salary of all elementary teachers is at present $2,433," reads the reply of the citizens committee. "The salary proposed by the committee would increase this average to $2,639. The average salary paid to men elementary teachers in 1910 was $1,318. Applying the index of the purchasing power of the dollar as contained in the United States Bureau of Labor Statistics, an average salary of $2,658 would have the same purchasing power in 1926 as had the man's average salary in 1910. The committee's schedule, therefore, lacks only $19 of giving to all elementary teachers, men and women, the purchasing power of the man's salary of 1910."

High School Group.

Comparing with the figures just cited the corresponding figures for senior high school teachers the committee continues:

"The present average salary of high school teachers is $3,293. The schedules proposed by the committee would increase this average to $4,229. The average salary of men high school teachers in 1910 was $2,143. Applying the index, an average salary of $4,322 would be required to restore the purchasing power of the man's high school teacher salary in 1910. In summation, the schedules proposed by the citizens committee come within $19 of restoring to all elementary teachers the man's salary of 1910. They fail by $93 to restore to the senior high school teachers the man's salary of 1910."

The committee takes cognizance of the fact that it has recommended a much larger increase for the high school teachers than for those in the elementary schools. But, it asserts, "this results from the committee's righting of the injustice done to the high school teachers in the legislation of 1919 and 1920, not from an underestimation of the very great importance of the elementary teachers' service."

In proof of this the committee states: "It would have required an increase of $1,029 in the present average salary of high school teachers to restore the purchasing power of the man's salary of 1910; it would have required an increase of only $225 to have restored to all elementary teachers the purchasing power of the man's salary of 1910."

Illegality Issue Removed.

These facts and figures the committee presents to refute the complaint that its recommendations discriminate against the kindergarten to 6B group in favor of those in the higher branches of the service. It assures the teachers that it has made "an honest effort to solve a complicated and confusing problem with entire impartiality in terms of the facts which are scientifically established," and it points out, moreover, that Dr. McGaughy, the director of the survey, is head of the department of elementary education at Teachers College.

Regarding the contention that the proposed schedules are contrary to law, the committee declares that in spite of the fact that it has been assured that the schedules are within the law it has changed the provision for annual increments from three increments of $120 and six of $180 to three of $132, three of $168 and three of $180, thus removing all criticism on the ground of illegality.

The committee accounts for the difference in increments between the regular maximum and the super maximum of elementary and other teachers by pointing out that the elementary teacher may attain the super maximum by one year of training in addition to the standard qualifications of three years beyond the high school course, while the junior and senior high school teachers must have a year of post graduate college work in order to qualify for the super maximum.

Editorials Selected from New York Papers Showing Unanimous Approval of Survey by the Citizens Committee

New York Times
May 15, 1926.

It is pertinent, however, to point out that work of the kind desired by the Mayor has for some time been under way. As the public knows, or ought to know, a Citizens' Committee on Teachers' Salaries has been voluntarily conducting inquiries. Its sole aim has been to ascertain the facts. If their proper interpretation calls for a higher level of pay for New York teachers, then that conclusion will be drawn. The belief is that if the people of this city are convinced that the system of public education is sound, and that they are getting their money's worth, they will be prepared to pay the larger sums that may be necessary. The Citizens' Committee has brought together for its investigation several experts, not only in education but in economics and statistics. One great purpose has been accurately to relate teachers' salaries to the increased cost of living. This is fundamental to the whole inquiry. What

New York Eve. Sun
May 17, 1926.

The expense of such an investigation would be justified if it were necessary. The question is wheth it is necessary. The Citizens Cor mittee on Teachers Salaries has be on the same job for months and h compiled a vast amount of inform tion preparatory to a final repo The personnel of the committ which includes ROBERT E. SIMON I JOHN H. FINLEY, Mrs. MOSKOWI PERCY S. STRAUS, LEE K. FRANKI ex-Senator LOCKWOOD and RAYMO

Brooklyn Eagle-May 15 1926.

Whatever the Governor does about the bills, the resolution of the Board of Estimate must not be allowed to act as a mere shelving of this problem. A committee of the United Parents Association proposes a sur-

New York Herald Tribune
May 15, 1926.

The readjustment should correspond accurately with the specific needs as determined by a complete survey of the complex situation.

For that purpose the Board of Estimate resolution sets up a committee of fifteen members, five to be appointed by the President of the Board of Education and ten by the Mayor. The committee is to make "a thorough and scientific study of the entire question of teachers' salaries in the City of New York." That is a sensible program, and it is precisely the one that is being carried out by the Citizens' Committee on Teachers Salaries organized last winter on the initiative of the United Parents' Associations. The executive members of that large and representative com-

New York Eve. Post
May 15, 1926.

WHEN the Committee of Fifteen which is to make a study of teachers' salaries is appointed in accordance with the resolution of the Board of Estimate it should ask itself just what its task is. To start at the beginning and investigate the whole question of what teachers receive and what they ought to receive will be to duplicate work which is already well advanced.

The Citizens Committee which was organized some months ago to collect facts bearing on teachers' salaries has

New York Evening World
May 17, 1926.

Under the circumstances, the decision of city and school officials to combine in creating a commission to make a diligent search for the solution of this perplexing problem is a step in the right direction. Fortunately, a committee of citizens has been at work along the same lines, gathering information

New York Morning World
May 17, 1926

TEACHERS' SALARIES

The Board of Estimate committee intrusted with the duty of investigating teachers' salaries is fortunate in having available for its information the McGaughy preliminary report and the other material already amassed and now being sought by the Citizens' Committee on Teachers' Salaries. Whether the city can afford to pay the rates

APPENDIX A

In this Appendix will be found the statistical tables which summarize many of the findings of the Citizens' Committee on Teachers Salaries. They are grouped here for purposes of easy reference and to make it possible to read the text of the report as a continuous story.

References to most of these tables and some explanations of them will be found in Chapter III - "The Facts Discovered". It is not possible, even in these detailed tables, to report more than a small part of the great mass of data secured by the Committee.

The data not here reported are on file, and available for reference, at the office of the Committee's Director, Professor J.R. McGaughy, Teachers College, Columbia University.

TABLE III

CHANGES IN COST OF LIVING IN NEW YORK CITY FROM DECEMBER 1914 to DECEMBER 1925.

Condensed from Table 2, page 68 of the Monthly Labor Review, Vol. XXII, No. 2, February 1926

Item of Expenditure	Per Cent of increase from December, 1914 to ---										
	Dec. 1915	Dec. 1916	Dec. 1917	Dec. 1918	Dec. 1919	Dec. 1920	Dec. 1921	Dec. 1922	Dec. 1923	Dec. 1924	Dec. 1925
Food	1.3	16.3	55.3	82.6	91.0	73.5	51.8	49.5	52.0	50.0	62.6
Clothing	4.8	22.3	54.2	131.3	219.7	201.8	117.8	98.3	102.7	97.7	95.9
Housing	1.1	1.1	2.6	6.5	23.4	38.1	53.7	56.7	62.4	67.1	69.5
Fuel and Light	1.1	11.0	19.9	45.5	50.6	87.5	90.7	95.7	94.2	93.3	126.0
House-furnishing Goods	8.4	27.6	56.5	126.5	172.9	185.9	132.0	121.6	131.5	119.4	110.4
Miscellaneous	2.0	14.9	44.7	70.0	95.8	116.3	116.9	111.6	113.5	116.7	118.2
All Items....	2.0	14.9	44.7	77.3	103.8	101.4	79.3	74.2	77.3	76.5	83.2

TABLE IV   INDEX NUMBERS SHOWING THE TREND IN THE RETAIL COST OF FOOD
IN THE UNITED STATES, BY YEARS, 1890 TO 1925*

This Table is Table 7 of the Monthly Labor Review, Page 16
of Vol. XXII, No. 2, February - 1926.
(Average for year 1913 = 100)

Year	Relative Price
1890	69.6
1891	70.6
1892	69.3
1893	71.0
1894	67.8
1895	66.5
1896	64.9
1897	65.4
1898	67.1
1899	67.7
1900	68.7
1901	71.5
1902	75.4
1903	75.0
1904	76.0
1905	76.4
1906	78.7
1907	82.0
1908	84.3
1909	88.7
1910	93.0
1911	92.0
1912	97.6
1913	100.0
1914	102.4
1915	101.3
1916	113.7
1917	146.4
1918	168.3
1919	185.9
1920	203.4
1921	153.3
1922	141.6
1923	146.2
1924	145.9
1925	157.4

*The number of articles included in the index number for each year has not been the same throughout the period, but a sufficient number have been used fairly to represent food as a whole. From 1890 to 1907, 30 articles were used; from 1907 to 1913, 15 articles; from 1913 to 1920, 22 articles; from 1921, 43 articles. The relatives for the period have been so computed as to be comparable with each other.

TABLE V.

RELATIVE PURCHASING POWER OF TEACHERS' SALARIES OF 1910 AND 1925
MEN TEACHERS OF NEW YORK CITY

Elementary and Junior High School	1910		1925		Average Salaries on 1910 Basis 1925	Index Number with 1910 as 100 1925
	Number of Teachers	Average Salary	Number of Teachers	Average Salary		
K to 6B	566	$1518	409	$1818	$901	68
7A to 9B	623	1850	292	3021	1498	81
Assistants to Principals	22	2400	71	3575	1772	74
Principals	220	3403	236	4718	2339	69
Teacher Clerks	5	1761	2	1750	867	49
Teachers of Atypical Children	2	1950	6	2121	1051	54
Junior High School	0	—	258	2920	1447	?
Grand Total	1258	$1978	1274	$2953	$1464	74
High School Principals	18	$5000	31	$6419	$3182	64
Clerical & Laboratory Assistants	10	1055	58	2066	1024	97
All Teachers	611	2143	1738	3384	1677	78
Grand Total	639	$2206	1827	$3393	$1682	76

TABLE VI.

RELATIVE PURCHASING POWER OF TEACHERS' SALARIES OF 1910 AND 1925
WOMEN TEACHERS OF NEW YORK CITY

Elementary and Junior High School	1910		1925		Average Salaries on 1910 Basis	Index Number with 1910 as 100
	Number of Teachers	Average Salary	Number of Teachers	Average Salary	1925	1925
K to 6B	10982	$ 913	14030	$2451	$1215	133
7A to 9B	1723	1288	2369	3145	1559	121
Assistants to Principal	386	1600	509	3585	1777	111
Principals	221	2338	281	4356	2159	92
Teacher Clerks	11	1280	728	1803	894	70
Teachers of Atypical Children	128	1104	761	3089	1531	139
Junior High School	0	---	1621	3090	1532	?
Grand Total	13451	$1006	20299	$2638	$1308	130
High School Principals	0	---	3	$6500	$3222	---
Clerical and Laboratory Assistants	13	845	143	2344	1162	138
All Teachers	676	1660	2326	3226	1599	96
Grand Total	689	$1644	2472	$3179	$1576	96

TABLE VII.

RELATIVE PURCHASING POWER OF TEACHERS' SALARIES OF 1910 AND 1925
MEN AND WOMEN TEACHERS OF NEW YORK CITY

Elementary and Junior High School	1910		1925		Average Salaries on 1910 Basis 1925	Index Number with 1910 as 100 1925
	Number of Teachers	Average Salary	Number of Teachers	Average Salary		
K to 6B	11348	$ 926	14439	$2433	$1206	130
7A to 9B	2346	1438	2661	3131	1552	108
Assistants to Principal	408	1643	580	3584	1777	108
Principals	441	2869	517	4521	2241	78
Teacher Clerks	16	1430	730	1803	894	62
Teachers of Atypical Children	130	1117	767	3081	1527	137
Junior High School	0	--	1879	3067	1520	?
Grand Total	14689	$1088	21573	$2657	$1317	121
High School Principals	18	$5000	34	$6426	$3185	64
Clerical and Laboratory Assistants	23	937	201	2263	1122	120
All Teachers	1287	1889	4064	3293	1632	86
Grand Total	1328	$1915	4299	$3270	$1621	85

TABLE VIII

INDEX FOR 1925 SALARIES BASED ON THE PURCHASING POWER OF THE 1900 DOLLAR

Elementary and Junior High School	Men's Salaries	Women's Salaries	Men's and Women's Salaries
K to 6B	50	98	96
7A to 9B	60	89	80
Assistants to Principal	55	82	80
Principals	51	68	58
Teacher Clerks	36	52	46
Teachers of Atypical Children	40	103	101
Junior High School	?		?
Grand Total	55	96	89
High School Principals	47	---	47
Clerical and Laboratory Assistants	72	102	89
All Teachers	58	71	64
Grand Total	56	71	63

TABLE IX

FACTS CONCERNING SALARIES IN NEW YORK CITY AND IN SIX OTHER AMERICAN CITIES
Reported Separately for Men and Women of Each Group

April - 1926

TEACHERS	Philadelphia	Cleveland	Detroit	St. Louis	Chicago	Kansas City	New York City	Sum of 6 Other Cities
Kindergarten								
No. of Men	0	0	0	0	0	0	0	0
No. of Women	191	193	210	202	543	119	1006	1458
% of Men	0	0	0	0	0	0	0	0
Av. Sal. of Men	-	-	-	-	-	-	-	-
Av. Sal. of Women	1836	2040	1899	1771	2238	1526	2527	0
Grades 1 - 6								
No. of Men	249	9	83	1297	83	80	409	507*
No. of Women	4450	2383	3018		5815	987	13024	16653
% of Men	5	½	3	?	1½	7	3	3
Av. Sal. of Men	1501	1955	2108	1913	2191	1910	1818	-
Av. Sal. of Women	1772		1872		2228	1714	2445	-
7 - 9th Grades Junior High School								
No. of Men	222	206	93	28	159	34	550	742
No. of Women	548	815	320	54	1428	111	3990	3276
% of Men	29	20	23	34	10	23	12	18
Av. Sal. of Men	2399	2200	2368	2204	2269	2090	2974	-
Av. Sal. of Women	2292		2317	2190	2423	1974	3123	-
Senior High School								
No. of Men	595	291	286	214	525	113	1738	2024
No. of Women	648	360	512	239	767	211	2326	2737
% of Men	48	45	36	47	41	35	43	43
Av. Sal. of Men	3070	2844	2537	2906	3208	2486	3584	-
Av. Sal. of Women	3033		2432	2734	3262	2149	3226	-
Atypical								
No. of Men	15	21	28	115	6	0	6	70*
No. of Women	403	294	219		23	20	761	959
% of Men	4	7	11	?	21	0	1	7
Av. Sal. of Men	1980	2200	2514	2201	2974	-	2121	-
Av. Sal. of Women	2160		2173		3162	1836	3089	-

* St. Louis is omitted.

TABLE IX(Con't)

FACTS CONCERNING SALARIES IN NEW YORK CITY AND IN SIX OTHER AMERICAN CITIES

PRINCIPALS	Philadelphia	Cleveland	Detroit	St. Louis	Chicago	Kansas City	New York City	Sum of 6 Other Cities
– Elementary Principals								
No. of Men	95	1	53	66	122	28	236	
No. of Women	102	106	108	23	148	46	281	
% of Men	48	1	33	74	45	38	46	
Av. Sal. of Men	3575	3087	3794	4158	4646	3337	4718	
Av. Sal. of Women	3483	3087	3451	3630	4591	2787	4356	
– Junior High School Principals								
No. of Men	9	8	9	2	4	3	**	
No. of Women	5	1	0	0	4	0		
% of Men	64	89	100	100	50	100		
Av. Sal. of Men	4806	3921	4933	4400	5200	4000		
Av. Sal. of Women	4700		–	–	4950	–		
Senior High School Principals								
No. of Men	9	13	11	6	22	5	31	
No. of Women	3	0	0	0	2	0	3	
% of Men	75	100	100	100	92	100	91	
Av. Sal. of Men	5500	4630	5364	5342	5673	4570	6419	
Av. Sal. of Women	5500	–	–	–	5300	–	6600	
Training School Principals								
No. of Men	2					1	2	
No. of Women	1					0	1	
% of Men	67					100	67	
Av. Sal. of Men	4500					4700	6500	
Av. Sal. of Women	4500					–	6500	

** Junior High School omitted.

TABLE IX (continued)
FACTS CONCERNING SALARIES IN NEW YORK CITY AND IN SIX OTHER AMERICAN CITIES

	Phila-delphia	Cleve-land	Detroit	St. Louis	Chicago	Kansas City	New York City	Sum of 6 other Cities
ADMINISTRATION OFFICERS								
Superintendent of Schools								
No. of Men	1	1	1	1	1	1	1	
Salary	12000	12000	125000	11000	15000	80000	20000	
Assoc. Supt. Schools								
No. of Men	4	4	4	5	4	2	7	
No. of Women	0	0	0	1	1	0	1	
% of Men	100	100	100	83	80	100	88	
Av. Sal. of Men	7000	6800	6225	7900	10000	4900	8250	
Av. Sal. of Women	-	-	-	8000	10000	-	8250	
District Superintendents								
No. of Men	9	3	3	2	9	3	25	
No. of Women	1	0	2	0	3	4	4	
% of Men	90	100	60	100	75	43	85	
Av. Sal. of Men	5389	5250	3933	5750	6500	4200	6539	
Av. Sal. of Women	5250	-	3750	-	6500	3365	6600	
Directors of Bureaus, etc.								
No. of Men	10	4	6	2	5			
No. of Women	3	1	2	0	1			
% of Men	77	80	75	100	83			
Av. Sal. of Men	5325	4533	2517	4450	5980			
Av. Sal. of Women	5333		3050	-	5500			
Supervisors								
No. of Men	43		47	12	5	6		
No. of Women	77		56	2	3	17		
% of Men	36		46	86	63	26		
Av. Sal. of Men	2687		2694	2765	5060	3218		
Av. Sal. of Women	2639		2902	3000	4667	2371		
Attendance Officers								
No. of Men	22	26		9		4	234	
No. of Women	62	22		10		3	74	
% of Men	26	54		47		57	78	
Av. Sal. of Men	1517	1872		1956		1400	2459	
Ave. Sal. of Women	1456			1960		1267	2294	

TABLE X . THE PROFESSIONAL PREPARATION OF NEW YORK CITY TEACHERS.

Summary of Facts Reported by 11081 Teachers, and Supervisory and Administrative Officers of the New York City Public Schools.

Groups	Number of Reports Received	Average Number of Years of Training:				Percent Having More Than Four Years Training Beyond High School Graduation.
		Beyond High School Graduation	In Teacher Training Institutions	In College or University (Under-Graduate)	In College or University (Post-Graduate)	
A. Kindergarten						
Women	354	2.2	2.0	0.0	0.0	16
Men	0	-	-	-	-	--
B. Grades 1 to 6						
Women	3856	2.5	2.0	0.0	0.0	19
Men	207	4.5	0.0	4.0	0.5	65
C. Elementary Unclassified						
Women	358	2.9	2.0	0.5	0.0	28
Men	96	3.8	1.0	2.7	0.0	45
D. Assistant Principals, Elementary						
Women	209	4.6	2.0	1.0	0.2	57
Men	52	6.1	2.0	4.0	1.6	84
E. Principals, Elementary						
Women	86	5.6	3.0	1.0	0.8	79
Men	108	6.1	0.0	4.0	1.5	86
F. Ungraded Classes						
Women	250	3.5	2.0	0.9	0.0	40
Men	9	4.4	1.0	3.6	0.1	75
G. Junior High, Grades 7, 8 and 9.						
Women	1235	3.4	2.0	0.8	0.0	37
Men	371	4.6	1.0	3.0	0.2	62
H. Assistant Principals, Junior High School						
Women	2	1.8	1.0	0.0	0.6	0
Men	4	4.8	1.0	4.0	0.0	100
I. Principals, Junior High School						
Women	4	6.1	2.0	0.0	1.6	100
Men	7	8.8	0.0	4.0	3.6	100
J. First Assist's. Heads of Dept's. Senior H.S.						
Women	55	5.2	2.0	4.0	0.9	76
Men	107	6.4	0.0	4.0	1.6	94
K. Assistants, Traditional Subjects						
Women	735	5.0	0.0	4.0	0.9	79
Men	683	5.7	0.0	4.0	1.3	90

TABLE X (Con't)

THE PROFESSIONAL PREPARATION OF NEW YORK CITY TEACHERS

Groups	Number of Reports Received	Average Number of Years of Training:				Percent Having More Than Four Years Training Beyond High School Graduation
		Beyond High School Graduation	In Teacher Training Institutions	In College or University (Under-Graduate)	In College or University (Post-Graduate)	
L. Assistants, Modern Subjects						
Women	518	4.4	2.0	2.5	0.0	57
Men	419	3.9	0.0	2.3	0.0	49
M. Assistants, Unclassified						
Women	104	4.9	1.0	4.0	0.6	76
Men	30	5.1	0.0	4.0	0.7	63
N. Clerical and Laboratory Assistants						
Women	40	1.5	0.0	1.0	0.0	29
Men	22	4.0	0.0	4.0	0.0	47
O. Assistant Principals, Senior H.S.						
Women	6	4.2	1.0	2.5	0.0	60
Men	27	5.9	0.0	4.0	1.6	96
P. Principals, Senior High School						
Women	1	5.6	1.0	4.0	0.6	100
Men	26	6.7	0.0	4.0	2.5	100
Q. District Supervisors						
Women	1	9.0	4.0	3.0	2.6	100
Men	3	3.6	-	4.0	0.0	0
R. District Superintendents						
Women	-	-	-	-	-	-
Men	6	7.1	2.0	3.0	2.5	100
S. Teachers Clerks						
Women	282	0.7	0.0	0.0	0.0	9
Men	4	3.5	0.0	4.0	0.0	33
T. Librarians						
Women	27	4.4	0.0	4.0	0.5	64
Men	4	2.6	2.0	0.6	0.4	25
U. Substitute Teachers						
Women	353	3.2	2.0	1.1	0.0	33
Men	98	4.5	0.0	4.0	0.5	66
V. Attendance Officers						
Women	64	0.6	0.0	0.1	0.0	9
Men	222	0.5	0.0	0.4	0.0	7

TABLE X (Con't)

THE PROFESSIONAL PREPARATION OF NEW YORK CITY TEACHERS

Groups	Number of Reports Received	Average Number of Years of Training:				Percent Having More Than Four Years Training Beyond High School Graduation
		Beyond High School Graduation	In Teacher Training Institutions	In College or University (Under-Graduate)	In College or University (Post-Graduate)	
All Women, Grand Total*	8540	3.0	2.0	1.6	0.0	33
All Married Women	1499	2.9	2.0	0.4	0.0	33
All Unmarried Women Living at Home	4202	2.9	2.0	0.5	0.0	29
All Unmarried Women Living away from Home	2333	3.5	2.0	0.9	0.0	41
All Men, Grand Total*	2505	4.9	0.0	4.0	0.6	68
All Married Men	1700	5.0	0.0	4.0	0.6	67
All Unmarried Men Living at Home	539	4.7	0.0	4.0	0.5	69
All Unmarried Men Living away from Home	171	5.1	0.0	4.0	0.7	70

* 506 Women and 95 Men did not report whether they were married or unmarried.

TABLE XI

AMOUNT OF TEACHING EXPERIENCE OF NEW YORK CITY TEACHERS

Summary of Facts Reported by 11061 Teachers and Supervisors and Administrative Officers of the New York City Schools
May - 1926

	Total	Total Years of Teaching Service		Percent Who Never Taught Outside of New York City
		Average	Range of Middle 50 Percent	
K - 6B				
Women	4569	9.7	4.7 to 19.0	87.3
Married	825	12.7	7.8 to 19.9	85.8
Unmarried Living at Home	2478	6.6	3.2 to 15.0	94.6
Unmarried Living Away from Home	979	18.9	10.9 to 26.9	68.5
Not Stated*	289	9.6	4.1 to 19.8	91.9
Men	303	4.3	2.5 to 9.7	88.6
Married	118	11.0	4.7 to 19.3	81.0
Unmarried Living at Home	157	2.8	2.1 to 4.6	94.9
Unmarried Living Away from Home	17	4.0	2.5 to 35.0	81.3
Not Stated*	11	4.8	3.3 to 8.0	90.0
JUNIOR HIGH SCHOOL AND GRADES 7 - 9				
Women	1235	19.1	11.5 to 26.9	84.7
Married	157	20.2	13.1 to 25.9	87.3
Unmarried Living at Home	579	15.1	9.2 to 22.9	92.1
Unmarried Living Away from Home	419	23.8	16.2 to 30.2	73.0
Not Stated*	80	19.8	12.3 to 28.2	87.0
Men	371	9.3	4.6 to 17.2	77.9
Married	265	11.2	5.8 to 18.9	74.3
Unmarried Living at Home	69	4.6	2.4 to 8.9	95.7
Unmarried Living Away from Home	25	8.5	4.1 to 20.5	56.0
Not Stated*	12	8.0	4.5 to 15.0	100.0
SENIOR HIGH SCHOOL				
Women	1357	16.0	8.9 to 23.7	57.2
Married	294	15.7	10.3 to 24.3	64.5
Unmarried Living at Home	492	11.1	5.9 to 18.7	72.0
Unmarried Living Away from Home	508	20.1	13.3 to 26.1	58.6
Not Stated*	63	17.0	9.3 to 25.3	70.0
Men	1132	13.7	7.4 to 22.2	65.9
Married	816	15.4	9.3 to 24.1	63.3
Unmarried Living At Home	186	6.7	4.3 to 10.8	82.2
Unmarried Living Away from Home	92	14.1	6.3 to 21.3	56.0
Not Stated*	58	15.0	10.9 to 23.3	64.9

* These persons reported their years of teaching service but not their economic status.

TABLE XI (Con't)

AMOUNT OF TEACHING EXPERIENCE OF NEW YORK CITY TEACHERS

	Total	Total Years of Teaching Service			Percent Who Never Taught Outside of New York City
		Average	Range of Middle 50 Percent		
TEACHERS OF ATYPICAL PUPILS					
Women	250	19.1	12.0	to 26.0	69.9
Married	46	20.8	13.2	to 25.8	72.7
Unmarried Living at Home	93	16.3	10.1	to 22.8	86.0
Unmarried Living Away from Home	98	21.8	13.4	to 25.8	72.7
Not Stated*	13	17.5	12.1	to 27.2	61.5
Men	9	6.7	3.4	to 9.7	55.6
Married	3	26.3	-	-	33.3
Unmarried Living at Home	4	-	-	-	50.0
Unmarried Living Away from Home	2	-	-	-	100.0
Not Stated*	-	-	-	-	-
All Women Teachers	7308	12.9	6.2	to 22.2	80.9
Married	1309	14.3	8.7	to 22.4	80.7
Unmarried Living at Home	3602	8.6	4.2	to 16.5	90.9
Unmarried Living Away from Home	1978	20.5	12.6	to 27.6	61.2
Not Stated*	419	13.5	5.4	to 23.1	87.0
All Men Teachers	1791	11.2	3.3	to 19.7	72.1
Married	1187	14.2	7.7	to 22.6	67.4
Unmarried Living at Home	412	4.6	2.6	to 8.2	88.9
Unmarried Living Away from Home	134	11.9	4.9	to 21.1	59.7
Not Stated*	58	12.3	5.2	to 18.6	76.3

*These persons reported their years of teaching service but not their economic status.

TABLE XII

DEPENDENTS OF CERTAIN GROUPS OF WOMEN TEACHERS CLASSIFIED AS TO ECONOMIC STATUS

Based on 1320 Married Women, 3641 Unmarried Women Living at Home, and 2005 Women Living Away from Home – A Total of 6966 Women Teachers

New York City – May, 1926

	Number Reporting	Percent Having Each Number of Dependents				
		1 or more	2 or more	3 or more	4 or more	5 or more
GRADES K – 6B						
Married Women	823	60	29	11	4	2
Unmarried Women Living at Home	2478	70	36	11	3	1
Women Living Away from Home	979	73	38	10	2	0
Total..................	4280	69	35	11	3	1
JUNIOR HIGH SCHOOL AND GRADES 7 – 9						
Married Women	157	70	35	8	1	0
Unmarried Women Living at Home	579	73	37	8	1	1
Women Living Away from Home	419	74	37	11	2	1
Total..................	1155	73	37	9	1	1
SENIOR HIGH SCHOOL						
Married Women	294	81	56	29	10	3
Unmarried Women Living at Home	491	68	35	9	2	0
Women Living Away from Home	509	70	32	8	1	0
Total..................	1294	72	38	13	3	1
TEACHERS OF ATYPICAL CHILDREN						
Married Women	46	77	41	11	0	0
Unmarried Women Living at Home	93	82	50	12	5	1
Women Living Away from Home	98	75	39	18	3	1
Total..................	237	78	43	14	3	1

TABLE XIII

RELATIONSHIP OF YEARS OF TEACHING SERVICE TO NUMBERS OF DEPENDENTS

Based on 6966 Women and 1754 Men Teachers of Elementary and Junior and Senior High Schools in New York City

May - 1926

	Years of Service	Number Reporting	Percent Having Each Number of Dependents				
			1 or more	2 or more	3 or more	4 or more	5 or more
Married Men	0 - 9	359	97	74	36	16	6
	10 - 25	610	98	84	57	27	10
More than	25	233	95	78	47	21	7
Total		1202	97	80	49	23	8
Married Women	0 - 9	416	50	24	7	2	1
	10 - 25	697	74	43	17	5	2
More than	25	207	75	42	21	10	4
Total		1320	66	36	15	5	2
Unmarried Men Living at Home	0 - 9	355	77	51	21	8	2
	10 - 25	74	80	38	16	3	2
More than	25	7	67	50	33	0	0
Total		416	77	49	20	7	2
Unmarried Women Living at Home	0 - 9	2112	67	35	11	.4	1
	10 - 25	1221	77	38	9	2	0
More than	25	309	72	35	8	1	0
Total		3642	71	36	10	3	1

TABLE XIII (Continued)

DEPENDENTS OF CERTAIN GROUPS OF WOMEN TEACHERS CLASSIFIED AS TO ECONOMIC STATUS

Years of Service	Number Reporting	Percent Having Each Number of Dependents				
		1 or more	2 or more	3 or more	4 or more	5 or more
Men Living Away from Home 0 - 9	59	71	39	12	10	2
10 - 25	57	73	47	18	4	2
More than 25	20	80	50	25	10	0
Total	136	73	44	17	7	2
Women Living Away from Home 0 - 9	362	74	37	12	2	1
10 - 25	1046	74	37	9	1	0
More than 25	596	70	35	11	2	1
Total	2004	73	36	10	2	1
All Men Teachers- 0 - 9	753	86	61	27	12	4
10 - 25	741	94	77	50	23	9
More than 25	260	93	75	45	19	6
Total	1754	91	70	40	18	6
All Women Teachers 0 - 9	2890	65	34	11	3	1
10 - 25	2964	75	39	11	3	1
More than 25	1112	71	36	12	3	1
Total	6966	70	36	11	3	1

TABLE XIV

RELATIONSHIP BETWEEN NUMBER OF CHILDREN AND NUMBER OF DEPENDENTS OF MARRIED MEN TEACHERS

Based on 1153 Married Men Teaching in Regular Day Schools in New York City

May - 1926

Number of Children	0	1	2	3	4	5	6	7+	Total	Percent of Married Men Having Dependents in Addition to Wife and Children
0	23	167	71	23	6				290	34.5
1	8	14	254	64	14				354	22.0
2	2	8	19	200	50	10	1	1	291	21.3
3	2	1	11	7	91	16	4		132	15.2
4		5	2	6	4	28	6		51	11.8
5		1			3	6	14	1	25	4.0
6							5		5	0.0
7								3	3	0.0
8								1	1	0.0
9								1	1	0.0
TOTAL	35	196	357	300	168	60	25	12	1153	23.2

TABLE XV

TEACHERS' EARNINGS FROM ALL SOURCES

Based on Reports from 1820 Men and 7158 Women Teachers in the Regular Day Schools of New York City, May, 1926

	Number Reporting	Average Total Earnings from all sources	Earnings from Outside Sources during Regular School Year		Earnings from Outside Sources During Summer Vacation	
			Per cent thus Employed	Average for those with Outside earnings	Per cent thus Employed	Average for those with Outside Earnings
Grades K – 6B						
Women						
Married	792	$2514	4	$318	1	$ 96
Unmarried Living at home	2393	2227	5	236	2	138
Unmarried Living away from home	951	2703	8	293	3	130
Not Stated*	248	2457	1	480	1	30
Total	4384	2395	5	270	2	130
Men						
Married	125	$2496	21	$553	7	$217
Unmarried Living at home	156	1882	22	309	10	180
Unmarried Living away from home	17	2662	6	450	6	300
Not Stated*	9	1861	0	---	11	150
Total	307	2175	20	415	9	197
JUNIOR HIGH SCHOOL AND GRADES 7 – 9						
Women						
Married	155	$3053	5	$244	0	---
Unmarried Living at home	570	2940	5	253	1	$1094
Unmarried Living away from home	404	3126	6	274	1	353
Not Stated*	72	3026	4	127	0	---
Total	1201	3022	5	254	1	724
Men						
Married	272	$3420	32	$682	12	$753
Unmarried Living at home	69	2853	33	695	10	269
Unmarried Living away from home	25	3010	16	475	12	142
Not Stated*	12	2808	17	800	8	350
Total	378	3270	31	680	11	622

*These persons reported their earnings but did not report their economic status.

TABLE XV - Continued

TEACHERS' EARNINGS FROM ALL SOURCES

	Number Reporting	Average Total Earnings from all Sources	Earnings from Outside Sources During Regular School Year		Earnings from Outside Sources During Summer Vacation	
			Per cent thus Employed	Average for those with Outside Earnings	Per cent thus Employed	Average for those with Outside Earnings
SENIOR HIGH SCHOOL						
Women						
Married	283	$3686	25	$843	7	$495
Unmarried Living at home	488	3007	9	426	4	206
Unmarried Living away from home	504	3410	11	379	3	232
Not Stated*	58	3207	3	188	2	110
Total	1333	3312	13	583	4	321
Men						
Married	811	$3974	33	$767	12	$560
Unmarried Living at home	186	2810	20	535	8	332
Unmarried Living away from home	92	3388	26	650	12	305
Not Stated*	37	3609	8	633	11	343
Total	1126	3722	29	731	12	506
TEACHERS OF ATYPICAL CHILDREN						
Women						
Married	43	$3027	2	$ 70	2	$250
Unmarried Living at home	90	2986	4	313	3	157
Unmarried Living away from home	95	3115	11	187	3	265
Not Stated*	12	2950	0	---	0	---
Total	240	3042	6	213	3	216
Men						
Married	3	$2483	0	---	0	---
Unmarried Living at home	4	2050	0	---	0	---
Unmarried Living away from home	2	2150	0	---	0	---
Not Stated*	0	---	0	---	0	---
Total	9	2206	0	---	0	---

*These persons reported their earnings but did not report their economic status.

TABLE XVI

THE RELATIONSHIP OF EARNINGS OF MARRIED MEN TEACHERS TO NUMBER OF CHILDREN IN FAMILY

Based on Reports from 1208 Married Men Teaching in Regular Day
Schools in New York City
May, 1926

	Number of Children	Number of Teachers Reporting	Average Total Earnings from all Sources	Earnings from Outside Sources During Regular School Year		Earnings from Outside Sources During Summer Vacation	
				Per cent thus Employed	Average for those with Outside earnings	Per cent thus Employed	Average for those with Outside Earnings
Grades K - 6B							
	0	62	$2137	21	$479	10	$266
	1	33	2820	24	703	3	80
	2	12	2867	17	375	8	60
	3	5	3430	60	591	20	222
	4	2	3250	0	---	0	---
	5	0	----	0	----	0	---
	6	1	2000	0	---	0	---
	7	1	2875	0	---	0	---
	Blank*	9	2383	0	---	0	---
Total	-	125	2496	21	553	7	217
Junior High School and Grades 7 - 9							
	0	63	$2826	22	$844	10	$363
	1	80	3371	34	510	13	500
	2	68	3660	35	653	4	1600
	3	30	3630	50	613	20	788
	4	14	4029	14	1820	21	467
	5	8	4263	38	367	25	2725
	6	0	----	0	---	0	----
	7	0	----	0	---	0	----
	8	1	3850	100	175	100	336
	Blank*	8	3812	13	4000	13	200
Total	-	272	3420	32	682	12	755
Senior High School							
	0	195	$3468	31	$619	10	$572
	1	247	3838	29	683	13	425
	2	213	4276	39	692	14	676
	3	98	4468	37	1316	14	299
	4	35	4407	34	886	17	1264
	5	17	4073	12	845	6	525
	6	4	3375	25	650	0	---
	7	2	4900	0	---	0	---
	8	0	----	0	---	0	---
	9	1	4250	100	800	0	---
	Blank*	5	4370	0	---	0	---
Total	-	811	3974	33	767	12	560

*These persons reported that they were married men but did not report the number of children in their families.

TABLE XVII

RENTS PAID AND SUB-RENTS RECEIVED BY NEW YORK CITY TEACHERS

Based on Report of 4071 Teachers of Regular Day Schools

May - 1926

	Teachers Who Do Not Sub-Rent Rooms		Teachers Who Do Sub-Rent Rooms		
	Number Reporting	Average Rental Paid	Number Reporting	Average Rental Paid	Average Sub-Rental Received
ELEMENTARY TEACHERS					
Women, Married	730	$ 910	40	$ 1047	$ 420
Women Living Away from Home	868	691	72	947	356
Men, Married	108	654	4	900	225
Men, Living Away from Home	16	-	-	-	-
TEACHERS OF GRADES 7 - 9 AND OF JUNIOR HIGH SCHOOL					
Women, Married	126	945	14	1100	429
Women Living Away from Home	357	778	44	1013	406
Men, Married	236	881	22	1100	350
Men, Living Away from Home	22	585	2	1000	475
SENIOR HIGH SCHOOL					
Women, Married	258	948	23	1450	450
Women Living Away from Home	417	757	74	1073	376
Men, Married	724	989	81	1369	448
Men Living Away from Home	86	752	5	1000	575
TEACHERS OF ATYPICAL CHILDREN					
Women, Married	39	969	4	1300	650
Women Living Away from Home	79	800	13	960	360
Men, Married	3	2	-	-	-
Men Living Away from Home	2	-	-	-	-

TABLE XVIII

RENTS PAID AND SUB-RENTS RECEIVED BY MEN AND WOMEN TEACHERS

Based on 114 Men and 285 Women Classified as to Economic Status

May - 1926

	Average	Range of Middle 50 Percent		
205 MARRIED WOMEN				
Rentals Paid	$ 992	$ 789	to	$1323
Sub-rentals Received	380	231	to	601
Difference	612	558	to	722
80 WOMEN LIVING AWAY FROM HOME				
Rentals Paid	1100	926	to	1675
Sub-rentals Received	439	270	to	639
Difference	661	656	to	1036
285 ALL WOMEN TEACHERS				
Rentals Paid	1021	822	to	1402
Sub-rentals Received	396	241	to	614
Difference	625	581	to	788
107 MARRIED MEN				
Rentals Paid	1295	1025	to	1689
Sub-rentals Received	412	256	to	659
Difference	883	769	to	1030
7 MEN LIVING AWAY FROM HOME				
Rentals Paid	1000	575	to	1538
Sub-rentals Received	550	281	to	725
Difference	450	294	to	813
114 ALL MEN TEACHERS				
Rentals Paid	1279	1008	to	1676
Sub-rentals Received	418	258	to	663
Difference	861	750	to	1013

TABLE XIX

RENTALS OF DIFFERENT TYPES OF HOUSING ACCOMODATIONS

Based on Facts by 1171 Married Men Teachers

May - 1926

ALL MARRIED MEN	Number Reporting	Annual Rentals Paid		
		Average	Range of Middle 50 Percent	
Furnished, Heated, Janitor Service	31	943	$697 to	$1213
Unfurnished, Heated, Jan. Serv.	430	869	737 to	1024
Unfurn., Not Heated, No Jan. Serv.	396	1113	887 to	1531
Furnished, Heated, No Janitor Serv.	3	650	350 to	800
Furnished, No Heat. No Jan. Serv.	1	1200	-	-
All Others	310	1010	819 to	1247
Total	1171	975	785 to	1214

TABLE XX

AVERAGE ANNUAL RENTALS PAID BY SEVERAL SALARY GROUPS
May - 1926

Salary Group	Married Teachers	Those Living at Home, not Married.	Those Living Away from Home.
Under $ 750	$ 859	$348	$461
$750 - 1499	754	384	538
1500 - 1999	800	396	566
2000 - 2499	821	510	670
2500 - 2999	911	564	720
3000 - 3499	925	684	778
3500 - 3999	1015	750	886
4000 - 4999	1115	792	1019
5000 - 5999	1281	720	1228
6000 - 7999	1441	672	877
8000 - and over	1691	510	----
Total	$4974	$522	$757

TABLE XXI

MONTHLY EXPENSE FOR MEALS

Based on 5658 Women and 1590 Men Teachers in the Regular Day Schools
of New York City

May - 1926

	Number Reporting	Monthly Expense for Meals	
		Average	Range of Middle 50 Percent
GRADES K - 6B			
Women			
Married	714	$ 85	$ 63 to 99
Unmarried Living at Home	1835	43	29 to 58
Unmarried Living Away from Home	870	75	43 to 81
Total	3419	52	38 to 79
Men			
Married	100	83	63 to 95
Unmarried Living at Home	134	37	22 to 41
Unmarried Living away from Home	17	54	40 to 80
Total	251	53	34 to 80
JUNIOR HIGH SCHOOL AND GRADES 7 - 9			
Women			
Married	132	85	52 to 102
Unmarried Living at Home	438	53	41 to 76
Unmarried Living Away from Home	375	65	48 to 85
Total	945	59	44 to 84
Men			
Married	245	92	74 to 119
Unmarried Living at Home	61	51	35 to 80
Unmarried Living Away from Home	23	64	40 to 109
Total	329	87	57 to 112
SENIOR HIGH SCHOOL			
Women			
Married	252	89	63 to 111
Unmarried Living at Home	382	50	37 to 73
Unmarried Living Away from Home	457	54	43 to 72
Total	1091	57	43 to 84
Men			
Married	768	95	79 to 147
Unmarried Living at Home	150	44	33 to 68
Unmarried Living Away from Home	85	67	50 to 88
Total	1003	90	67 to 115

TABLE XXI(Con't)

MONTHLY EXPENSE FOR MEALS

	Number Reporting	Monthly Expense for Meals	
		Average	Range of Middle 50 Percent
TEACHERS OF ATYPICAL CHILDREN			
Women			
Married	41	89	72 to 104
Unmarried Living at Home	74	56	43 to 87
Unmarried Living Away from Home	88	67	48 to 87
Total	203	71	47 to 92
Men			
Married	1	93	- -
Unmarried Living at Home	4	43	26 to 73
Unmarried Living Away from Home	2	48	- -.

TABLE XXII

RELATIONSHIP OF NUMBER OF CHILDREN TO MONTHLY EXPENSE FOR MEALS

Based on 1113 Married Men Teachers in the Regular Day Schools of New York City

May - 1926

Number of Children	Grades K - 6B		Junior High School Grades 7 - 9		Senior High School	
	Number Reporting	Average Expense	Number Reporting	Average Expense	Number Reporting	Average Expense
0	51	$ 75	52	$ 79	183	$ 84
1	28	82	78	89	236	100
2	12	98	64	99	197	100
3	5	89	29	100	95	112
4	2	90	13	132	34	121
5	0	-	8	133	16	142
6	1	93	0	-	4	135
7	1	150	0	-	2	150
8	0	-	1	150	0	-
9	0	-	0	-	1	150
TOTAL	100	$ 83	245	$ 92	768	$ 95

TABLE XXIII

RENTS PAID BY SEVERAL TEACHING GROUPS
Based on Reports from 1,621 Men and 5,992 Women Teachers in Regular Day Schools of New York City. May, 1926

	Number Reporting	Average Annual Rental
GRADES K - 6B		
Women		
Married	770	$919
Unmarried Living at Home	1934	Less than $200
Unmarried Living away from Home	942	$707
Total	3646	Less than $200
Men		
Married	112	$664
Unmarried Living at Home	116	Less than $200
Unmarried Living away from Home	16	$475
Total	244	Less than $200
JUNIOR HIGH SCHOOL AND GRADES 7 - 9		
Women		
Married	140	$945
Unmarried Living at Home	444	Less than $200
Unmarried Living away from Home	401	$807
Total	985	$477
Men		
Married	253	$907
Unmarried Living at Home	59	Less than $200
Unmarried Living away from Home	23	$650
Total	335	$813
SENIOR HIGH SCHOOL		
Women		
Married	281	$965
Unmarried Living at Home	380	Less than $200
Unmarried Living away from Home	491	$805
Total	1152	$669
Men		
Married	805	$1012
Unmarried Living at Home	159	Less than $200
Unmarried Living away from Home	91	$757
Total	1055	$936
TEACHERS OF ATYPICAL CHILDREN		
Women		
Married	43	$994
Unmarried Living at Home	74	Less than $200
Unmarried Living away from Home	92	$827
Total	209	$650
Men		
Married	1	$1000
Unmarried Living at Home	4	Less than $200
Unmarried Living away from Home	2	$500
Total	7	Less than $200

APPENDIX B

SUMMARY OF THE STRAUSS RICCA BILL OF 1926

At a number of places in the preceding chapters of this report of the Citizens' Committee on Teachers' Salaries references have been made to the salaries proposed in the Strauss Ricca Bill presented to the State Legislature in the spring of 1926. A summary of the proposals of that bill and of the schedules at present in operation in New York City are presented in this Appendix.

This is the second of the two so-called Ricca Bills proposing increased salaries for teachers. The first of these bills was passed by the Legislature in the spring of 1925 and was vetoed by Governor Smith. The bill which is summarized in this Appendix was likewise passed and vetoed in the spring of 1926.

It will be remembered that these bills, and the schedules which they would have made effective, were drawn by representatives of the teacher organizations of New York City. Further discussion of this legislation will be found in Chapter I, page

TABLE XXIV

STRAUSS-RICCA BILL
SALARY SCHEDULES FOR NEW YORK CITY TEACHERS
ELEMENTARY SCHOOLS

License	Present Schedules	Ricca Bill Proposals
K - 6B	$1500. 11 x 125 $2875	$1600. 2 x 135 9 x 170 $3400.
7A - 9B	$1900. 9 x 150 $3250.	$2100. 2 x 160 7 x 200 $3820.
Asst. to Principal	$3400. 2 x 100 $3600.	$3900; 3 x 200 $4500.
Principal	$3750. 4 x 250 $4750.	$5100. 3 x 300 $6000.
Teacher Clerks	$1200. 7 x 100 $1900.	$1300. 11 x 125 $2675.
Substitutes	$5.20 per diem	$8.00 per diem
Teachers of day Classes in English and Citizenship		1st 3 yrs. $2.50 - $2.00 per hr. After three yrs. $3.00 - $2.50 per hr.
Senior Teachers Pupil Teachers		$300. bonus $3. per diem
Teachers of atypical pupils	$1900. 9 x 150 $3250.	$2120. 2 x 165 7 x 210 $3920.
Junior High School	$1900 9 x 150 $3250.	$2100. 2 x 160 7 x 200 $3820.

TABLE XXIV

STRAUSS-RICCA BILL (continued)

HIGH SCHOOLS

License	Present Schedules	Ricca Bill Proposals
Principal	$6500.	$7000. 2 x 375 $7750.
First Ass't.))) Senior) High Assistant) School) Teachers	$3200. 5 x 200 $4200. $1800. 12 x 150 $3700.	$4500. 3 x 250 $5250. $2150. 2 x 200 8 x 225 $4350.
Clerical and Laboratory Assistants	$1500. 12 x 100 $2700.	$1500. 12 x 125 $3000.
Substitutes	$6.50 per diem	$10.00 per diem
Home teachers of crippled children		1st 3 yrs. - $8.00 after 3 yrs. - $11.00

EVENING HIGH AND TRADE SCHOOLS

Teachers	$6.50	$7.00 2 x .50 $8.00
Assistant to Principals	$6.50	$8.50
Clerical, Laboratory and Library Assistants	$3.90	$5.50
Principals and Supervisors	$9.10	$11.00

EVENING ELEMENTARY SCHOOLS

Teachers on probationary appointment	$4.50	$5.50
on permanent appointment	$5.50	$6.50

TABLE XXIV

EVENING ELEMENTARY SCHOOLS
(continued)

License	Present Schedules	Ricca Bill Proposals
Teachers in Charge, Fewer than Twelve Classes	$5.20	$7.50
Teachers in Charge, Twelve or More Classes	$6.50	$8.00
Principals and Supervisors	$7.80	$9.50
General Assistants		Probationary appointment $5.50
		Under permanent appointment $6.50

VACATION HIGH SCHOOLS

Teachers	$8.00	$9.50
Asst. to Principal		$5.00 per summer session
Principals		$7.00 " " "
Clerical Assistants		$6.00

VACATION ELEMENTARY SCHOOLS

Teachers	$3.90	$5.50 1st 3 yrs. $6.50 after 3 yrs.
Assistants to Principal		$8.00
Principals	$5.85	$9.00
Supervisors	$7.80	$10.00

COMMUNITY CENTERS AND VACATION PLAYGROUNDS

Supervisors	$7.80	$10.00
Principals	$5.20	$8.50
Teachers	$3.25	$5.50 1st 3 yrs. $6.50 after 3 yrs.

TABLE XXIV.

COMMUNITY CENTERS AND VACATION PLAYGROUNDS
(continued)

License	Present Schedules	Ricca Bill Proposals
Assistant Teacher Librarian and Pianist		$4.00 1st 3 yrs. $5.00 after 3 yrs.
Teachers of Swimming and in Charge of Baths.	$3.90	$6.00 1st 3 yrs. $7.00 after 3 yrs.
Substitutes	$1.95	$3.25

AFTERNOON ATHLETIC CENTERS

Teacher		$5.50
Supervisors		$6.50

Printed in Dunstable, United Kingdom